RAPIDITY

TIME MANAGEMENT ON THE DOT

DEJI BADIRU

RAPIDITY
TIME MANAGEMENT ON THE DOT

iUniverse books may be ordered through booksellers or by contacting:

iUniverse
1663 Liberty Drive
Bloomington, IN 47403
www.iuniverse.com
844-349-9409

Because of the dynamic nature of the Internet, any web addresses or links contained in this book may have changed since publication and may no longer be valid. The views expressed in this work are solely those of the author and do not necessarily reflect the views of the publisher, and the publisher hereby disclaims any responsibility for them.

Any people depicted in stock imagery provided by Getty Images are models, and such images are being used for illustrative purposes only. Certain stock imagery © Getty Images.

ISBN: 978-1-6632-3265-6 (sc)
ISBN: 978-1-6632-3266-3 (e)

Library of Congress Control Number: 2021924837

Print information available on the last page.

iUniverse rev. date: 12/08/2021

Adedeji Badiru writes as the primary author for ABICS Publications (www.abicspublications.com), A Division of AB International Consulting Services, dedicated to publishing books for home, work, and leisure.

ABICS Publications
A Division of
AB International Consulting Services (ABICS)

www.ABICSPublications.com

Books for home, work, and leisure

Books in the ABICS Publications book series, published by iUniverse, Inc., on recreational, educational, motivational, and personal development books, include the titles below:

Rapidity: Time Management on the Dot

Physics of Skateboarding: Fun, Fellowship, and Following

The Twenty-Fifth Hour: Secrets to Getting More Done Every Day

Kitchen Project Management: The Art and Science of an Organized Kitchen

Wives of the Same School: Tributes and Straight Talk

The Rooster and the Hen: Story of Love at Last Look

The Story of Saint Finbarr's College: Contributions to Education and Sports Development in Nigeria

Physics of Soccer II: Science and Strategies for a Better Game

Kitchen Dynamics: The rice way

Consumer Economics: The value of dollars and sense for money management

Youth Soccer Training Slides: A Math and Science Approach

My Little Blue Book of Project Management

8-by-3 Paradigm for Time Management

Badiru's Equation of Student Success: Intelligence, Common Sense, and Self-discipline

Isi Cookbook: Collection of Easy Nigerian Recipes

Blessings of a Father: Education contributions of Father Slattery at Saint Finbarr's College

Physics in the Nigerian Kitchen: The Science, the Art, and the Recipes

The Physics of Soccer: Using Math and Science to Improve Your Game

Getting things done through project management

CONTENTS

WHAT IS RAPIDITY?

The title of this book was selected deliberately to convey the urgency often associated with time management. To do something rapidly is to get it done within reason, on time, and within the available resources.

Rapidity, as presented in this book, facilitates making and executing project decisions on a fast track. In ordinary parlance, rapidity is a noun denoting the attribute of doing something with great speed. Some thesaurus options for rapidity are swiftness, quickness, speed, speediness, briskness, expeditiousness, dispatch, alacrity, promptness, and immediacy. Rapidity, as a conveyor of time management on the dot, implies an alignment of time, cost, and quality of getting things done.

My goal of writing this book is to provide tips and guidance for getting more done each day through a more effective use of time. Time saved translates to time gained. Thus, the concept of creating additional virtual hour in the day presents the essence of using every minute more effectively. Managing time requires dedication and commitment. Occasional drifting away from time-management goals is okay, but a wholesale abandonment of the lessons learned in this book will be a disservice to personal pursuits and the mission of time management.

CHAPTER 1

PANDEMIC-DRIVEN TIME MANAGEMENT

"What is worth doing is worth doing well
and worth doing promptly."
– Adedeji Badiru

Tempus fugit

"Tempus fugit" is a Latin phrase, usually translated into English as "time flies." It is reported as first appearing in The Georgics, a poem by Latin poet, Virgil, published circa 29 BCE. It appears in the poem on line 284 of book 3 as "fugit inreparabile tempus," which translates to "it escapes, irretrievable time." It is this reverence to time as "flying away" that motivated my poem on time, which is presented in the opening segment of Chapter 2.

Time management on the dot, the theme of this book, means doing the right thing, at the right time, in the right measure, and at the appropriate performance level. If performance is not on the dot, we get a misalignment of efforts and resources.

What COVID Has Wrought

The COVID-19 pandemic caused more havoc and anxiety than anyone ever imagined could happen over a short period of time. In spite of the disruptive and destructive power of the pandemic, new opportunities emerged to challenge our society on what we do, how we do it, where we do it, when we do it, and why we do it. The common element running through all the challenges is time. Time is the basis for performance by who does what when. Due to the pandemic, the nature of work has changed forever. How we work has also changed and will continue to change. Even if the pandemic disappears tomorrow (an unlikely scenario), what we have learned, in terms of coping and working under a cloud of the pandemic, will be with us for years to come. The beneficial aspect of that is that we have discovered new ways of managing our time to do the variety of things that have surfaced to be done in response to the pandemic. Activities that we were not performing routinely prior to the pandemic are now common elements of our daily routines whether at work, home, or leisure. Wearing masks, sanitizing hands, soap-washing hands, and maintaining social distancing create additional activities requiring additional consciousness of time. Even tasks that, individually, consume very little time can become destabilizing for well-laid plans of getting things done. Consequently, better time management skills are needed by everyone. I have been fortunate to be able to adapt my pre-pandemic time-management approaches to the shifting landscape of getting things done during the pandemic. Hopefully, this adaptive practice will prevail in the post-pandemic era. In this book, my goal is to share my time-management approaches with the readers. Even in the pandemic-disrupted operating environment, we can still find reasons and techniques for managing our time more efficiently and effectively.

Beyond the pandemic-driven need for better time management, my motivation for writing this book at this time is based on the common question that is often posed to me regarding how I am able to get a lot done each day with little or no visible indication of time panic. My simple and consistent answer is about how I, adaptively, use structured time and activity management to make an effective use of my limited time. Basically, I eliminate or minimize fluff from my activities. Using rigorous project management, I always explore and assess if and how I can run concurrent activities without necessarily multitasking. Machine or technology-operated activities are perfect for coordinating with other manual activities. Some good examples are baking an item in the oven while doing laundry. These are two totally unrelated household chores. Yet, they can be choreographed to take place at the same time under watchful and attentive eyes. Watching TV while writing a manuscript is another favorite approach for getting my writing tasks done while keeping up with essential news. At work, I prefer hallway impromptu discussions that get things decided and moving forward rather than scheduling separate meetings time to accomplish the same thing. In fact, I have an adverse view of regularly-schedule meetings because of the extra unproductive times that precede and follow a meeting. I refer to such times as "set-down" time and "re-setup" time. A meeting that starts at 2pm will often require you to disengage from productive activities by 1:30pm because you need time to "set down" whatever you are doing in time to make your way to the meeting. This explains why some people always run late to meetings, if they don't account for the required set-down time in their calendars. At the other end (after the meeting), more time is needed to reengage with productive activities. In this regard, I once wrote an article about "My perspectives on meetings." It goes as follows:

Meetings represent one avenue for information flow and knowledge sharing for group decision-making. Effective management of meetings is an important skill for any administrator. Unfortunately, meetings often degenerate to time-wasters; consequently obstructing productivity and detracting from other essential functions. This is because most meetings are irrationally scheduled, poorly organized, improperly managed, or even unnecessary. In some organizations, meetings are conducted as a matter of routine requirement rather than necessity. While meetings are essential for communication and decision-making, they accomplish nothing if they are not managed properly. A meeting of 30 people wasting only 30 minutes, in effect, wastes 15 full hours of productive time. That much time, in any organization, can amount to thousands of dollars in lost productivity. It does not make sense to use a one-hour meeting to discuss a task that will take only five minutes to perform. This is analogous to hiring someone at an annual salary of $100,000 to manage an annual budget of $5,000.

In 1993, a newspaper columnist and humorist, Dan Stewart, commented about management meetings:

"Management meetings are rapidly becoming this country's biggest growth industry. As nearly as I can determine, the working day of a typical middle manager consists of seven hours of meetings, plus lunch. Half a dozen years ago at my newspaper, we hired a new middle management editor with an impressive reputation. Unfortunately, I haven't met her yet. On her first day at work, she went into a meeting and has never come out." Stewart concludes his satire with "I'm expected to attend the next meeting. I'm not sure when it's scheduled exactly. I think they're having a meeting this afternoon about that."

Conceptually, in the past, when an employee had a request, he went to his boss, who would say "yes" or "no" right away. The whole process might take less than one minute out of the employee's day. Nowadays several hierarchies of meetings may be needed to review the request. Thus, we may have a departmental meeting, a middle management staff meeting, upper management meeting, executive meeting, steering committee meeting, ad hoc committee meeting, an off-site retreat, and a meeting with outside consultants; all for the purpose of reviewing the simple request. Mind you, some meetings are still needed in organizations. The goal is to only schedule them when needed and manage them effectively. In some cases, even poorly-managed meetings are still need to satisfy our needs as social animals. In such meetings, there may be values in dragging on and socializing over chips and drinks. My point is that whatever meetings we have should be managed effectively, time-wise. My perspectives on time-wasting meetings are echoed in the contents throughout this book. Effective time management is the cornerstone of productivity at home, at work, or at leisure.

CHAPTER 2

A POEM ON THE FLIGHT OF TIME

"Avoid hurried worries in harried times."
– Adedeji Badiru

The Flight of Time

What is the speed and direction of time?
Time flies; but it has no wings.
Time goes fast; but it has no speed.
Where has time gone? But it has no destination.
Time goes here and there; but it has no direction.
Time has no embodiment. It neither flies, walks, nor goes anywhere.
Yet, the passage of time is constant.
© 2006, Deji Badiru

Time is going. As such, we must use whatever time we have more productively.

Time is fascinating, both in our physical world as well as in the science of physics.

What is time?

"Time is the most unknown of all unknown things."- Aristotle

In spite of its unknown characteristics, we all depend on time to get things done in our daily lives.

Once time is gone, it is gone. In the physical sense, time moves in only one direction. But in physics, time could be viewed as being all-encompassing and amorphous, as if it flows from multiple directions under the second law of thermodynamics. Without getting too technical, let us consider the *arrow of time*, which in physics, is the theory of the one-way direction of *time*. The thermodynamic *arrow of time* is provided by the second law of thermodynamics, which says that in an isolated system, entropy (disorder) tends to increase with *time*. Entropy is a measure of the capacity of a system to undergo disordering change spontaneously. This is why disorder is always increasing in our daily lives . . . and we do not have full control of time.

The unanticipated occurrence of COVID-19 in the 2019/2020 timeframe is a good example of a disorder in our, otherwise, orderly existence.

We don't really have an isolated system in our everyday lives. In the science of physics, there is no perfectly closed system. Every system interacts with its environment in one way or another. The fast spread of COVID-19 is indicative of how interconnected we are all over the world. Nothing stands still for any length of time. That is disorder! Entropy! In our universe, the disorder is constantly happening. In the context of this book, time disruption is constantly happening, through accidental occurrences, deliberate acts of sabotage, or human mismanagement. In a relatable context of this assertion, within the short duration of writing this particular paragraph, my time was disrupted several times. My spouse wanted to ask me an important question. Uninvited notifications sounded about new postings on WhatsApp social media. The TV blasted the latest news flash. The central heating system kicked in with a sound that momentarily diverted my attention. My mobile phone rang. An errant Advertisement flashed on my computer screen. The noise of a passing vehicle attracted my attention to look through the window to check what was happening. So, the entropy (disorder) in my writing effort increased. So, my time got misaligned and I faced the risk of a time mismanagement. It was only through a refocusing that I could regain my time control.

In our typical time-management efforts, we do not have a perfect control of our time. Things in our environment will always interact with us to upend whatever time-management plans we may have. So, a more rigorous and explicit effort must be made to control whatever time is at our disposal.

The resolution approach of this book is to create more time virtually rather than physically. Although time is incompressible, we can, indeed, squeeze more outputs out of whatever limited time we have. Rather than seeking to control time in direction or space, we should seek to control how we use time to accomplish more and more things. If we can get more things done within a confined time boundary, then we have created a virtual time to do more things.

Each human being, from the time of birth, will always be confronted with more and more things to do. Yet, the available time is not going to expand. Technically, this means there is always more to do than there is time to do them all. So, we desire more time. Unfortunately, each day is pegged, physically, at only 24 hours. Thus, a virtual twenty-fifth hour is needed, according to Badiru (2020). Going further more aggressively, a determined reader can even squeeze out a virtual 26th hour (or more) out of each day.

One of the primary reasons we don't get as much done each day is that time is used and abused in irrational ways. To get more done each day, we need to use time more efficiently and more effectively. That is the premise of this book on time management on the dot.

If we had more time, we could get more done each day. Time is incompressible and the only way to get the twenty-fifth hour in a day is to create it virtually. In the context of this book's premise, the twenty-fifth hour of the day is created virtually through saving time throughout the day. The quotes below enjoin us to use time more productively to accomplish more outputs.

"You may delay, but time will not." - Benjamin Franklin

"If only I had just one more hour in the day, I could get it done." – Generic voice of a laggard.

The above generic regret is a common chagrin of those who have been time-vanquished. The secret to having that one more extra hour is to create it virtually by saving it from other engagements, particularly the unproductive and non-value-adding ones.

As the saying goes, time keeps moving on. It waits for no one. Since time is physically incompressible, the only way to create more time is to do it virtually through common-sense cautious usage of time and simple applications of business tools and techniques. A reckless usage of time can only lead to needing more time to get things done. The theme of this book is to help readers learn how to use limited time more efficiently and effectively. The goal is to have a virtual creation of time by saving time. Because time is the underlying factor and platform over which we accomplish tasks, it should be respected and worshipped as a sacred asset.

To create time is to save time. We should always strive to move time from an area of wasteful usage to an area of productive usage. The different ways to save time in order to get more done is what this book is all about, as conveyed by its title. I am often asked how I manage to do so many diverse things without being a jack of all trades. My simple answer is that I always respect my time and I strive to put it into a good use each and every time.

Not having enough time to do whatever we want to do is a common complaint of the society. This has become even more pronounced under the COVID-19 pandemic. This book records managing time on the dot, proactively. The common problem of time management is that we focus too much on time that we already have instead of managing the time that we don't yet have. In this regard, preemption of typical time robbers is the approach recommended by this book. This means virtual time creation. This is time savings that can be redirected to new and value-adding tasks.

Strategies for Saving Time

Engage in projects that, even if they cost you a little time up front, can save you recurring time later on. These can be as simple as minor household-chore-saving projects. One good example for preempting repeated cleaning of soiled floor in the so-called mud room at the garage entrance of a house is the use of a stone-filled shoe tray. A stone-filled shoe tray is simply a receptacle filled with pebbles. Mudded-up kids' shoes go into the receptable instead of on the floor. The less floor cleaning the homeowner has to do, the more time could be available for other useful pursuits.

Deji Badiru's 8-by-3 Paradigm

- Are you constantly pressed for time?
- Do you always wish you had more time to do all that you have to do?
- Are you always pressed to meet deadlines?
- Are you facing challenges in balancing your work life and your home life?
- Do you often find yourself rushing to complete your errands?
- Are multiple priorities keeping you disoriented?
- Do you face the futility of getting organized?

If you answer affirmatively to any of these questions, Deji Badiru's 8-by-3 Paradigm for Time Management (Badiru, 2013) can help you in many areas of time endeavor. The paradigm, which is published as a separate title in the ABICS Publications book series, presents the trick of getting things done on time by finding a formula for balancing both competing and complementing priorities. The pursuit of personal goals requires efficient time management. This is exactly what the 8-by-3 paradigm offers and it can help with the virtual creation of more time.

The overarching theme of the 8-by-3 paradigm of time management is to view time as the basis for everything we do. An efficient use of time is the foundation for success in all endeavors. Balancing time implies using explicit and equitable allotments of time to the various undertakings of each day, thus virtually creating more time. undertakings. The three blocks of time in the 8-by-3 paradigm cover the following:

- Work activities (Basis for livelihood)
- Home/leisure activities (Basis for life balance)
- Sleep time (Basis for a healthy living)

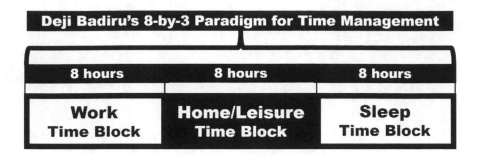

Each block has sub-blocks that are managed in contiguous hierarchical timeline templates. With a target audience of working adults, the 8-by-3 paradigm can be customized for each person's specific needs and circumstances. The paradigm does not require sacrificing one time block for another or vice versa. Rather, it encourages balancing time across work time, home time, and leisure time because all three are essential for a complete and fulfilling life, whereby more virtual time is created to get more done across the spectrum of activity priorities.

By using the 8-by-3 paradigm for time management, one can focus on hierarchical allotment of time to three major blocks of human activities during a 24-hour day. As with any imprecise management scenario, there are no strict demarcation lines between the three 8-hour blocks of time. There is a continuity of time segments throughout the day. This sense of continuous involvement is often the source of poor management of time by most people. In the 8-by-3 paradigm, the idea is to adopt a conceptual segmentation of the day into three distinct, but contiguous 8-hour blocks of time, each with its own level of output accountability. Transitional overlapping of the time blocks is allowed to include time for regular professional or career work (8 hours), time for discretionary domestic and/ or recreational activities at home (8 hours), and time for recuperative sleep (8 hours). Any virtual time that can be saved (created) to supplement the above blocks of time fits the categorization of creating the twenty-fifth hour of the day.

It should be noted that sleep is an explicitly-scheduled requirement in the 8-by-3 paradigm. If sleep is not treated as a schedulable item, it becomes easily compromised and sacrificed in the usual race against time with respect to the competing demands on our time. Sleep should be treated as a high-priority requirement, whose allotment of time must be preserved. Occasional incursion into the sleep block of time is okay, as long as it does not become a habitual practice. Excessive borrowing from sleep time is like engaging in deficit spending. It will eventually catch up with the offender in terms of degradation of health. Personal wellbeing affects how well we use our time. So, we must invest in healthy pursuits. A healthy person is a more time-efficient person. There is always more to do than there is time to do. We can do more if we are healthy, prudent, and disciplined. The time invested in health upfront will save time later on and contribute to the virtual creation of the twenty-fifth hour of the day. Sustaining each 8-by-3 block of time means being efficient and effective with the activities in each block. Crunch-time problems can be avoided by following the suggestions below:

- Give each task its own allocation of one of the 8-by-3 blocks of time.
- Embrace every task within its own block of time.
- Dedicate a block for every task and a task for every block.
- Avoid unnecessary low-value activities that rob time.
- Reserve daytime hours for what needs to be done during daylight.
- Do not do during one block of time what is best done in another block of time.

"There is time for everything, and a season for each activity." – Ecclesiastes 3:1

For those engaged in education rather than a paid employment, the education requirement should be handled as a deliberate work engagement with all the rights and dedication of the 8-by-3 time allocation. For those combining work and school, the 8-by-3 paradigm is still applicable and effective for balancing work, school, and home times.

Email time management

Time management within the work life is essential for the overall wellbeing of a person. If work time is managed effectively, there will be a reduced need for work to encroach upon home life. The major time robbers at work are frivolous pursuits, chitty-chatty (chit-chat) engagements, and proliferation of back-and-forth emails. Generating, opening, reading, and replying to emails consume much of the time of workers. Email usage has become a part and parcel of the evolution of human communication, not only in the office environment, but also in home and community engagements. The social media is awash in back-and-forth precursory communication, albeit to the detriment of tangible accomplishments. Since we cannot avoid it, we should find ways to manage it, with respect to time efficiency, thereby facilitating the virtual creation of the twenty-fifth hour of the day.

Some tips for managing emails are presented below:

- To reduce receiving emails, you need to reduce sending more emails. Each email sent invites one or more emails that must be dealt with, thereby consuming more precious time.
- Don't send an email unless you really need to.
- Delete emails promptly if they don't need to be saved. Saved emails require more time to manage, review, sort, and deal with later on.
- Avoid Reply-All, if not needed. Replying to all creates opportunities for "All" to send you more and new emails, thereby requiring you to spend more time responding.
- Keep emails brief. Longer emails proliferate and re-germinate to consume more time.
- Use brief subject-line-only emails, if possible, to get your point across. Think of a twitter-type communication. This approach is great for "Thank you" notes.
- Use EOM (End of Message) on subject lines to indicate no need to open the email body if the subject line adequately conveys the essence of the communication, thus saving email-handling time.

Family time management

The home life is the essence of our life. Managing the home life effectively leads to happiness and contentment. The home life is a reflection of what makes us who we are. At home, we engage in a wider variety of activities than in a typical work environment. The diversity of the home life can range from a single household, a married household, a childless household, a single-kid household, a single-parent household, a multiple-kids household, and a roommate household to an extended-family household. Each one requires different approaches to managing the relevant tasks, goals, and objectives. Even the physical structure of the house can impact how time is managed in the household. For example, single-family houses, condos, and apartment complexes may imply different approaches to managing time based on influences and interactions with other individuals. In a single household, just as in a multiple-person household, comparative benchmarks of how others handle certain chores may affect how you manage your own chores. I have always argued that siblings within the same age range growing up in the same household create developmental benchmarks and examples for themselves. Managing time in home-life chores may benefit from the following tips 8-by-3 paradigm tips:

- Allocate sufficient time for family interactions.
- Identify desirable family-time activities, such as eating together, group outing, sports, watching favorite TV programs, watching movies, visiting, and vacation travel.
- Use the kitchen as a frequent congregation point for the family. So, keep it organized, comfortable, and accessible.
- Establish family traditions early. Later-year establishments are more difficult and require more time.
- Communicate family values to everyone. It saves time by avoiding corrective pursuits later on.
- Establish an assignment of home chores and tasks upfront. This helps manage task execution .time later on.
- Allocate family time at the earliest opportunity because time invested early saves time in the long run
- Make a commitment to execute assigned chores promptly.
- Dedicate time to each item that has to be done. Letting an item drift consumes more time in the attempt to find a slot for it.
- Limit serendipitous reception of unannounced family engagements.
- Keep the family block to be the family block, recognizing that occasional cannibalizing of time from one 8-by-3 block to another may become necessary, but it should be done within reason.

Sleep time management

It is generally believed that we spend between 25% and 35% of our life sleeping. This is based on a total overall life assessment. The times, obviously, vary on a day-by-day basis, depending on what is going on in each day. The recommended amount of sleep per day is eight hours, which is 33.33% of the day. Although rarely do we accomplish this on a day-by-day basis, it is important to recognize and preserve that block of the day. This is one of the main premises of the 8-by-3 paradigm for time management. If this block of time is consistently compromised, it can lead to adverse effects on health and wellbeing. This detrimental impact may be so gradual that the individual hardly notices it. When health issues do develop later on, it is difficult to trace them back to the long-term effect of sacrificing sleep. Each person's genetic makeup does influence reactions to sleep patterns. There are morning people and there are late-night people. But, by and large, over a long stretch of time, having a sufficient sleep is crucial for each category of people. Occasional needs may necessitate waking up too early or sleeping extremely late. If these are balanced out by occasional compensatory sleep, things should even out over time. If you are a morning person, use the morning hours for the most tasking activities. Don't wake up early just for the sake of waking up early. Do something worthwhile in the early waking hours. Below are some tips for ensuring adequate sleep under the 8-by-3 paradigm of time management:

- Make sleep a priority, just as you would any other high-priority requirement.
- End work when work needs to be ended.
- Establish a specific time to go to bed, with plus or minus allowances, as may be needed.
- Go to bed early if you are an early riser, it may be the only way to ensure you sleep long enough.
- Put everything else aside and focus on a restful sleep when it is your time to sleep.
- Don't attempt to perform a function requiring a high level of cognition and concentration when you are sleepy. For example,

sleeping while driving leads to many fatal accidents annually. The National Sleep Foundation (www.sleepfoundation.org) reported in 2009 that 1.9 million drivers have fatigue-related car crashes or near misses each year in the USA. No doubt, each accident causes those involved an enormous loss of time, if not loss of life. Sleep deprivation causes loss of time in terms of requiring more time to perform tasks, thereby negating the virtual twenty-fifth hour of the day.

Leisure time management

Leisure time provides an opportunity to recuperate and rejuvenate the body, soul, and mind. Balancing leisure time with the other time essentials makes for a complete, rewarding, and gratifying existence. We should not overindulge in leisure or any of the other essentials. Leisure time should be distinguished from time for business, work, or household chores, although a careful choreographing can overlap leisure with the other essentials. The 8-by-3 paradigm for time management facilitates an explicit allocation of time spent away from work and home-based domestic chores, even if overlapping becomes unavoidable. My own leisure activities include reading, writing, cooking, painting, and dancing. Reading printed newspapers is one of my highly-coveted daily leisure activities. Cooking, as listed here, does not represent an undertaking as a domestic chore, but rather as an object of relaxation and culinary experimentations, which are gratifying for me. It also creates an opportunity for being a kitchen member of the household, which is another aspect of family togetherness. Don't consider leisure time as idle time or wasted time if it is fulfilling its intended purpose. Leisure time that is properly managed can contribute to the creation of the virtual twenty-fifth hour of the day.

Time and ethics

A violation of ethics will come back to consume time later on in terms of the need for a corrective or punitive action. Abiding by ethics in the first place will save time later on, thereby contributing to the creation of the virtual twenty-fifth hour of the day.

Using the 8-by-3 paradigm of time management has the desirable side effects of upholding good work ethics and abiding by ethical standards. With respect to good work ethics, personal morality and work responsibility should be inculcated into time management practices. Taking accountability for what needs to be done rather than taking evasive or defensive paths will result in good outcomes both in the short term as well as the long term. Whining is a time robber. Constructive whining may be necessary in some cases to bring a problem to the attention of leadership, with an offer of a solution option. Destructive whining wastes time without offering a solution to the prevailing problem. With respect to ethical standards, the code of ethics of a relevant profession can help uphold and advance the integrity, honor, and dignity of the person. Many professions offer rigorous codes of ethics that individuals may draw upon. Work ethics and ethical standards directly influence physical wellbeing, mental alertness, teamwork, sportsmanship, wingman-ship, selflessness, and leadership in ways that lead to efficient utilization of time, thereby making it possible to achieve the virtual creation of the twenty-fifth hour of the day.

The 8-by-3 paradigm of time management conveys the concept of balancing time over the three general categories of home, work, and leisure. While a strict adherence to time blocking may not be possible always, it is expected that the paradigm can serve as a continual reminder of the importance of balancing time requirements, thus making it possible to create the virtual twenty-fifth hour of the day. The benefits to be obtained from this approach include the following:

- Balancing time allocations for work, home, and leisure activities
- Balancing competing and complementing priorities
- Reducing search time for items in the home or office
- Reducing time for household chores
- Getting organized for more efficient chores at home or office
- Straightening out personal goals with respect to time allocations
- Recognizing the constant passage of time
- Becoming proficient with time-cost tradeoffs

- Allocating time efficiently across multiple objectives
- Taking drudgery out of household chores
- Conserving energy in the pursuit of tasks
- Getting family together for fun and fellowship projects
- Minimizing labor-intensive run around when executing tasks

Chapter 2 References

1. Badiru, Deji (2020), **The Twenty-Fifth Hour: Secrets to Getting More Done Every Day**, iUniverse, Bloomington, IN.
2. Badiru, Deji (2013), *8-by-3 Paradigm for Time Management: Balancing Work, Home, and Leisure*, iUniverse, Bloomington, Indiana, USA.

CHAPTER 3

TIME EFFICIENCY AND EFFECTIVENESS

"Patchwork never works."
– Adedeji Badiru

An efficient usage of time implies an ability to virtually create additional time. If time is used efficiently and more effectively, more virtual time would be possible, thereby creating the virtual twenty-fifth hour of the day.

Efficient management of time matters a lot, from the standpoint of personal and professional development. It is not how much time you have that is important, but how well you use the time that you have.

We talk much about saving money and accumulating wealth. But we don't commit as much emotion and energy to saving time and accumulating accomplishments. From a resource standpoint, time is money. Therefore, saving time is as essential as saving money.

Every minute counts, just as every dollar counts in our personal pursuits. Time waits for no one.

A lot of fluff exists in our day-to-day activities. Oftentimes, those who claim not to have enough time to do what needs to be done are those who mismanage time the most. If fluff can be removed from our activities, more time will be virtually created to accomplish additional meaningful pursuits. It is important to get busy and stay busy. Time is used more efficiently when there is more to do. Idle time is frittered away unproductively. When fully loaded with tasks, we are forced to manage our time more carefully. Otherwise, we will be tempted to postpone and defer activities, with the end result that not as much is accomplished time wise.

It is important to identify and highlight the time implications in everything we do. If time is managed tactically, we can succeed with almost everything. Time is precious in the sense that it is through time that we accomplish our goals and objectives. Time is irrecoverable in the sense that time, once lost, cannot be regained. Time is incompressible in the sense that the passage of time itself is fixed, even though the time-based duration of a task may be condensed or elongated. Time is relative, in the sense that different people use time differently with different contexts.

Getting things done on a daily basis is a matter of efficient allocation of time and resources. Time, as a limited commodity, must be utilized efficiently. Resources, as a scarce asset, must be managed effectively. Urgent items are treated as urgent and executed promptly to get them out of the way. This requires forsaking procrastination and vacillation every time a temptation to put things off develops. Important items are scheduled and done at the earliest convenient timeframe.

There is a time factor in everything we do. Even a simple activity such as conserving water has eventual time implications. For example, the more gallons of water you use, the higher your water bill will be. The higher your water bill is, the more work you have to do to earn enough money to pay the higher water bill. The more money you have to earn, the more time you will need to work to earn the money. So, time utilization is the end result. Consequently, conserving water, in addition to its environmental benefits, does have time-saving implications for the individual person. This is an extreme example, but it typifies the premise of good time management. The same rationale can be applied to other human challenges, such as preventive maintenance of a vehicle, cooking in batches rather than in spurts, and using clean-as-you-go housekeeping practices. If you love to cook for gatherings, you don't have to cook for every gathering. You may occasionally use precooked items from a grocery store. You may cook for every other gathering or so, such that the audience can still appreciate your cooking prowess and special recipes. Large-scale cooking for every gathering every time consumes a lot of time and may distract you from other high-value time-sensitive goals. The key is to reduce the number of time-consuming chores that may lead to a rushed pursuit of other high-value engagements. Haste makes waste and can result in reworks that are time costly.

One accomplishment a day puts 365 accomplishments within reach in one year. This is plenty of room to do what you need to do. So, don't whine about time; get going with time management. Time efficiency enhances your chances for professional success and it emphasizes your commitment to excellence.

Haste Equates to Waste

More time is wasted doing things over than doing them correctly in the first place. More time taken upfront to do something well the first time saves a lot more time later on. Errors happen when we allow haste to creep into our activities. Such errors then require time to correct, thereby encroaching on the time allotted for the next activity. The correction time constitutes a waste and should be minimized. Always give yourself some wiggle room. Getting yourself in a tight corner will cost you more time.

Preemption Is Better than Correction

Preempting problems can avoid the need for disruptive corrective actions later on. A key aspect of managing the time blocks is to strictly control what goes in each block in the first place. By preempting potential problems, we can conserve precious time to allow us to perform each task within its reasonable block of time. The common saying below emphasizes this point:

> "If you don't have time to do it right the first time,
> when would you have time to do it over?"

Productivity at the Hands of Time

Whatever we do and produce is at the mercy of time. Take time to use time wisely, promptly, and productively. Unnecessary procrastination is nothing more than deferring accountability and responsibility. There is never a better time to perform a task than at its first opportunity. Procrastination does not give you more time. It simply gets things cramped up later on. Activities should be done when they come up to be done. Each missed opportunity leads to deficit scheduling of pending activities. Very much like deficit spending, procrastination puts a person in the situation of having to play catch up. Do what you must when you first have the time to do it. You may not have a subsequent opportunity to do it. The following quotes are pertinent in this regard:

"Only put off until tomorrow what you are
willing to die having left undone"
- Pablo Picasso

"You cannot escape the responsibility of
tomorrow by evading it today."
- Abraham Lincoln

A related tip from this book is to exercise time-based productivity by not doing in the dark what is best done in daylight hours. This has implications for both safety and productivity. Doing certain things in the dark can pose more risks for safety and security.

Likewise, don't waste productive daylight hours on items that can alternately be done in later hours of the day. By human body clock, 4 a.m. has been found to be a less productive time of the day to do any meaningful work. The body's functionality and productive capability tend to be markedly diminished at 4 a.m. in the morning. This is partly or wholly due to the body's natural *circadian rhythm.*

The circadian rhythm is a 24-hour internal clock that runs cerebrally in the background of human consciousness in cycles between sleepiness and alertness at regular intervals. It is often referred to as the sleep/wake cycle. Bigger swings in the circadian rhythm occur when a person is more sleep-deprived. This is where the efficacy of the 8-by-3 paradigm is essential for overall work productivity.

Time Value of a Minute

What is your minute worth? When people ask you to do something that only takes a couple of minutes, be sure to consider how much your "couple of minutes" is worth. Serendipitously committing a minute here and a couple of minutes there will result in a lot of your time going down the drain and intractable. Another important aspect of time assessment is to recognize how much an engagement actually costs you. A one-hour meeting often will cost you a lot more than one hour, considering the additional time requirements to disengage from what you were doing before the engagement and the extra time needed to get back to speed after the engagement ends. I refer to these additional boundary times as "set-down" time and "re-ramp-up" time. Using this principle, it can be seen that a one-hour engagement can consume a lot more time because of the pre and post time requirements. Many people don't account for these extra times and they end up wondering why not much gets done in an average work day. When I invite many people to a meeting or a gathering, I am always conscious of the collective time of the group. So, I endeavor to use the collective time efficiently and effectively. The sum of minutes from the work times of several high-salaried employees can amount to a significant productivity loss and dollars unaccounted for.

Time efficiency, effectiveness, and productivity usually go hand-in-hand. An integrated definition of each is essential to identify where improvement can be pursued. The usual business techniques for improving efficiency, effectiveness, and productivity are quite amenable for personal adaptation.

What is Efficiency?

Efficiency refers to the extent to which a resource (time, money, effort, etc.) is properly utilized to achieve an expected outcome. The goal, thus, is to minimize resource expenditure, reduce waste, eliminate unnecessary effort, and maximize output. The ideal (i.e., the perfect case) is to have 100% efficiency. This is rarely possible in practice. Usually expressed as a percentage, efficiency (e) is computed as output divided by input:

$$\text{Efficiency} = \text{output}/\text{input} = \text{result}/\text{effort}$$

What is Effectiveness?

Effectiveness is an ambiguous evaluative term that is difficult to quantify. It is primarily concerned with achieving objectives. To model effectiveness quantitatively, we can consider the fact that an "objective" is essentially an "output" related to the numerator of the efficiency equation above. Thus, we can assess the extent to which the various objectives of an organization are met with respect to the available resources. Although efficiency and effectiveness often go hand-in-hand, they are, indeed, different and distinct. For example, one can forego efficiency for the sake of getting a particular objective accomplished. Consider the statement "if we can get it done, money is no object." The military, by virtue of being mission driven often operates this way. If, for instance, our goal is to go from point A to point B to hit a target, and we do hit the target, no matter what it takes, then we are effective. We may not be efficient based on the amount of resources expended to hit the target. For the purpose of this paper, a cost-based measure of effectiveness is defined as follows:

Measure of Effectiveness on interval [0, 1] = Level of satisfaction of the objective on a scale [0, 1] divided by the cost of achieving the objective expressed in pertinent cost basis: money, time, measurable resource, etc.

If an objective is fully achieved, its satisfaction rating will be 1. If not achieved at all, it will be zero. Thus, having the cost in the denominator gives a measure of achieving the objective per unit cost. If the effectiveness measures of achieving several objectives are to be compared, then the denominator (i.e., cost) will need to be normalized to a uniform scale. Overall system effectiveness can be computed as a composite summation of all the effectiveness measures.

Because of the potential for the effectiveness measure to be very small based on the magnitude of the cost denominator, it is essential to scale this measure to a scale of 0 to 100. Thus, the highest comparative effectiveness per unit cost will be 100 while the lowest will be 0. The above quantitative measure of effectiveness makes most sense when comparing alternatives for achieving a specific objective. If the effectiveness of achieving an objective in absolute (non-comparative) terms is desired, it would be necessary to determine the range of costs, minimum to maximum, applicable for achieving the objective. Then, we can assess how well we satisfy the objective with the expenditure of the maximum cost versus the expenditure of the minimum cost. By analogy, killing two birds with one stone is efficient. By comparison, the question of effectiveness is whether we kill a bird with one stone or kill the same bird with two stones, if the primary goal is to kill the bird nonetheless. In technical terms, systems that are designed with parallel redundancy can be effective, but not necessarily efficient. In such cases, the goal is to be effective (get the job done) rather than to be efficient. Productivity is a measure of throughput per unit time. The traditional application of productivity computation is in the production environment with countable or measurable units of output in repetitive operations. Typical productivity formulas include the following:

$$\text{Productivity} = \text{Output Quantity/Input Quantity}$$
$$\text{Productivity} = \text{Efficiency/Utilization}$$

Performance management and output assessment are essential for determining efficiency and effectiveness of actions. As the opening quote above suggests, you cannot wish away problems. Problems must be identified, confronted, and controlled. Since the focus of the 8-by-3 paradigm is on using time more efficiently, it is important to understand what efficiency implies and how to assess it so that control actions can be taken if necessary. Performance can be defined in terms of several specific metrics along different axes. Examples are efficiency, effectiveness, and productivity, which usually go hand-in-hand. The common business techniques for improving efficiency, effectiveness, and productivity are quite amenable for personal adaptation. Efficiency refers to the extent to which a resource (time, money, effort, etc.) is properly utilized to achieve an expected outcome. The goal, thus, is to minimize resource expenditure, reduce waste, eliminate unnecessary effort, and maximize output. The ideal (i.e., the perfect case) is to have 100% efficiency. This is rarely possible in practice. Usually expressed as a percentage, efficiency is computed as the ratio of output over input. That is, efficiency is output divided by input or result divided by effort. This ratio is also adapted for measuring productivity. For the purpose of improving personal efficiency, the 8-by-3 paradigm defines operational efficiency as follows: Operational efficiency involves a scenario, whereby all individuals coordinate their respective activities, considering all the relevant factors, such that the overall personal goals can be achieved with symbiotic input-process-output relationships with the minimum expenditure of resources yielding maximum possible outputs.

Effectiveness is a nebulous evaluative term that is difficult to quantify. It is primarily concerned with achieving the specific objectives, which constitute the broad goals of an organization. To model effectiveness quantitatively, we can consider the fact that an "objective" is essentially an "output" related to the numerator of the efficiency equation. Thus, we can assess the extent to which the various objectives of an individual are met with respect to the available resources. Although efficiency and effectiveness often go hand-in-hand, they are, indeed, different and distinct. For example, one can forego efficiency for the sake of getting a particular objective accomplished. Consider the statement "if we can get it done, money is no object." Emergency cases often operate this way. If, for instance, our goal is to go from point A to point B to accomplish an objective, and we do achieve the objective, no matter what it takes, then we are effective. We may not be efficient based on the amount of resources expended to achieve the objective. For the purpose of this book, a cost-based measure of effectiveness is defined as the level of satisfaction divided by the cost of achieving that satisfaction. The measure of effectiveness is within the interval of zero to one, level of satisfaction of the objective is rated on a scale of zero to one, and the cost of achieving the objective is expressed on a pertinent cost basis, such as money, time, measurable resources, and so on.

If an objective is fully achieved, its satisfaction rating will be one. If not achieved at all, it will be zero. Thus, having the cost in the denominator gives a measure of achieving the objective per unit cost. If the effectiveness measures of achieving several objectives are to be compared, then the denominator (i.e., cost) will need to be normalized to a uniform scale. The overall personal effectiveness can be computed as a summation of the normalized effectiveness of each of the various objectives. Because of the potential for the effectiveness measure to be very small based on the magnitude of the cost denominator, it is essential to scale the above measure to a scale of 0 to 100. Thus, the highest comparative effectiveness per unit cost will be 100 while the lowest will be 0. The above measure of effectiveness makes most sense when comparing alternatives for achieving a specific objective. If the effectiveness of achieving an objective in absolute (non-comparative) terms is desired, it would be necessary to determine the range of costs, minimum to maximum, applicable for achieving the objective. Then, we can assess how well we satisfy the objective with the expenditure of the maximum cost versus the expenditure of the minimum cost. By analogy, "killing two birds with one stone" is efficient. By comparison, the question of effectiveness is whether we kill a bird with one stone or kill the same bird with two stones, if the primary goal is to kill the bird nonetheless. In personal management terms, pursuits that are implemented with parallel redundancy can be effective, but not necessarily efficient. In other words, a backup arrangement or a contingency plan may not be efficient, but could be effective.

In such cases, the goal is to be effective (get the job done) rather than to be efficient.

What is Productivity?

Productivity is a measure of accomplishment (throughput) per unit time. The traditional application of productivity computation is in the production environment with countable or measurable units of output in repetitive operations. Manufacturing is a perfect scenario for productivity computations. In the home environment, for example, a productivity measure may pertain to how many meal servings can be produced within one hour. Typically, productivity is represented as output quantify divided by the input quantity. Applying the utilization percentage to this ratio modifies the ratio to provide an actual productivity yield. For the personal environment, which is a non-manufacturing setting, productivity analysis is still of interest. The home environment is composed, primarily, of family members, relatives, and friends, whose productivity must be measured in alternate terms, perhaps through personal work rate analysis. A simple measure of group or team output is represented as productivity multiplied by the level of effort. Productivity is expressed as a yield per person-time while effort is represented as duration times the number of people. Efficiency, effectiveness, and productivity are not simply a matter of resource availability. A person or an organization with ample resources can still be inefficient, ineffective, and unproductive. Thus, personal impediments and obstacles, apart from resource availability, should be identified and mitigated. This can be done with respect to each person's hierarchy of needs. Examples of self-inflicted impediments are ambiguous goals, undefined objectives, and unrealistic expectations. Managing one's blocks of time using the 8-by-3 paradigm can help in resolving the problem of getting many things done efficiently and effectively.

CHAPTER 4

LEAN PRINCIPLES FOR TIME MANAGEMENT

"If you want to get there faster, you should start earlier."
– Adedeji Badiru

Corporate tools that are routinely used for managerial functions in business, industry, government, military, and academia are also applicable and useful for personal-level time management. For example, in the discipline of industrial engineering, tools, such as Lean Principles, are used extensively. The key elements of the practice of industrial engineering are people, processes, and products with a focus on optimum performance and continuous improvement, often in allocating scarce resources. The goal is always to achieve an integrated process of the applications of various tools and approaches for improving operations while reducing resource expenditures. Continuous process improvement is an on-going systematic effort to improve day-to-day operations to remain productive and operationally efficient. Productivity, quality of service, process enhancement, flexibility, adaptability, work design, schedule optimization, and cost containment are within the scope of the objectives any organization, even if they are under the banner of different monikers. Increases in operational efficiency are best accomplished through gradual and consistent closing of gaps rather than the pursuit of one giant improvement step. The practice of drastic or sudden improvement impedes process optimization goals. As we do in the corporate environment, so we can do in our daily management of time.

What is Lean?

We are not talking about a lean and fit person here. Lean, in the context of organizational process improvement, means the identification and elimination of sources of *waste* in operations. By comparison, six-sigma involves the identification and elimination of sources of *defects* through the reduction of variability. When lean and six-sigma are combined, an organization can reduce both waste and defects in operations. Consequently, the organization can achieve higher performance, better employee morale, more satisfied constituents, and more effective utilization of limited resources, thus saving time in the long run. That is the spirit of time management on the dot, as espoused by this book.

The basic principle of lean is to take a close look at the elemental compositions of a process to eliminate non-value-adding elements (or movements). Lean and Six Sigma techniques use analytical and statistical techniques as the basis for pursuing improvement objectives. But the achievement of those goals depends on having a structured approach to the activities associated with what needs to be done. If an IE approach is embraced at the outset in military operations, it will pave the way for achieving Six Sigma results and make it possible to realize lean outcomes. The key in any operational management endeavor is to have a structured plan so that diagnostic and corrective steps can be pursued. If inefficiency is allowed to creep into military operations, it would take much more time, effort, and cost to achieve a lean Six Sigma cleanup. To put the above concepts in a military perspective, six-sigma implies executing command and control processes such that errors are minimized in the long run. Likewise, the technique of lean ensures that only value-adding command

and control actions are undertaken. In applying a lean concept approach, being able to keep operations within control means avoiding unnecessary motions and actions. This means the elimination of waste. This brings to mind **Parkinson's Law** of bureaucracy, which states that "work expands to fill the time available," as a result of which unnecessary activities are performed. Military leaders must ensure that functions do not extend needlessly just to use up available time and resources. Short and effective functions are better than protracted ones that result in counterproductive results.

The mushrooming of social media can create an inefficient use of time due to chaotic interjection of social discussions into our social order. Referring back briefly to the concept of entropy discussed in Chapter One, we can see an analogy to the absence of lean operations. In thermodynamic terms, the entropy of an object is a measure of the amount of energy which is unavailable to do work. In this sense, entropy is a measure of uncertainty, randomness, and disorder in a system. This is akin to the growing prevalence of social media in our society.

The growing usage of social media is such that there are not enough hours in the day to keep up with all the postings. Many postings can be disruptive, interruptive, and disorienting. Time disorder increases with social media. Therefore, fits the concept of entropy, which can lead to a tendency to procrastinate.

Procrastination Wastes Time

Anticipation of deadline problems and taking action proactively in advance of the looming delay could be viewed as being "pre-crastination" as opposed to procrastination. By the same analogy, "post-crastination" can be viewed as doing something after the deadline has passed, thus rendering the action ineffective, unacceptable, or no longer relevant.

Haste makes waste.
Rush makes errors.
Errors require more time to correct or redo.

Slowing down to smell the roses is the usual call to take your time and get the job done well. Slowing down can be beneficial for getting things done well the first time around.

You can be a "procrastinator" without getting to the edge of rushing. Doing things too far in advance can lead to not gathering all the relevant information adequately before executing action.

No decision is ever perfect. Depending on the problem situation, check if you can live with a less-than-perfect solution. Is a 95-percent solution good enough compared to 100-percent solution? If so, there is no need to create additional non-lean activities that do not add any new value. The process of arriving at a decision can be prolonged, many times, for no justifiable reason. You should decide on your action and move forward. Eighty-percent of the time, your first decision is the right decision. Dilly-dallying on a decision only consumes more time unnecessarily.

CHAPTER 5

SIX SIGMA FOR TIME MANAGEMENT

"Invest ten minutes of proper planning to
get one hour of time savings."
– Adedeji Badiru

Work time can be saved by exercising consistency of actions. In production systems, this consistency is pursued through the technique of six sigma. Of course, in personal activities, we would not be instituting rigorous six-sigma processes. However, to whatever extent possible, we should be practicing consistent routines. A consistent routine will minimize incidents of re-dos (repeats) and re-runs.

What is Six Sigma?

"A bad system will defeat a good person every time." - Deming

Six Sigma is often combined with Lean Principles as complementary tools. Lean focuses on waste reduction while Six Sigma focuses on variation reduction. Lean uses mostly qualitative tools while Six Sigma uses mostly quantitative techniques in identifying and rectifying sources of variation in processes and activities. It is important to note that a lack of consistency in personal activities can lead to ineffective utilization of time, particularly in terms of doing repairs, redoing work, and recovering from errors. Thus, we can use Six Sigma to achieve better time management. Six Sigma is best defined as a business process-improvement approach to reduce variation. The more consistent a process is, the more likely the product will meet quality expectations. The technique seeks to find and eliminate causes of defects and errors, reduce cycle times, reduce costs of operations, improve productivity, meet customer expectations, achieve higher asset utilization, and improve return on investment (ROI). If we can reduce or remove re-runs, we can get more done each day. Thereby, creating the illusion of having the twenty-fifth hour in the day. Six Sigma deals with producing data driven results through management support of the initiatives. Six Sigma pertains to sustainability because without the actual data, decisions would be made on trial and error. Sustainable environments require having actual data to back up decisions so that methods are used to have improvements for future generations. The basic methodology of Six Sigma includes a five-step method approach that consists of the following:

1. **Define:** Initiate the project, describe the specific problem, identify the project's goals and scope, and define key customers and their Critical to Quality (CTQ) attributes.
2. **Measure:** Understand the data and processes with a view to specifications needed for meeting customer requirements, develop and evaluate measurement systems, and measure current process performance.
3. **Analyze:** Identify potential cause of problems, analyze current processes, identify relationships between inputs, processes, and outputs, and carry out data analysis.
4. **Improve:** Generate solutions based on root causes and data driven analysis while implementing effective measures.
5. **Control:** Finalize control systems and verify long-term capabilities for sustainable and long-term success.

The goal for Six Sigma is to strive for perfection by reducing variation and meeting customer demands. The customer is known to make specifications for processes. Statistically speaking, Six Sigma is a process that produces 3.4 defects per million opportunities. A defect is defined as any event that is outside of the customer's specifications. On a statistical scale, one sigma is represented by the Greek letter s (sigma), which marks the distance on the horizontal axis between the mean (m) and the inflection point of the bell curve (normal curve). The greater the distance, the greater is the spread of values encountered and the less consistency is possible in the system.

In a plot of a six-sigma process, the areas under the normal curve within different ranges around the mean would be indicated. The upper and lower specification limits (USL and LSL) are plus or minus three sigmas from the mean or within a six-sigma spread. Because of the properties of the normal distribution, values lying as far away as six sigmas from the mean are rare because most data points (99.73%) are within three sigmas from the mean, except for processes that are seriously out of control. When a process is out of control, more inconsistencies creep in and more time is spent getting things right. Thus, more virtual time (beyond 24 hours) may be needed.

Six Sigma allows no more than 3.4 defects per million parts manufactured or 3.4 errors per million activities in a service operation. To appreciate the effect of Six Sigma, consider a process that is 99% perfect (10,000 defects per million parts). Six Sigma requires the process to be 99.99966% perfect to produce only 3.4 defects per million, that is 3.4/1,000,000 = 0.0000034 = 0.00034%. That means that the area under the normal curve within six sigma is 99.99966% with a defect area of 0.00034%. The following tools are the most common Six-Sigma tools.

- Project Charter
- SIPOC
- Kano Model
- CTQ
- Affinity Diagram
- Measurement System Analysis

- Gage R and R
- Variation
- Graphical Analysis
- Location and Spread
- Process Capabilities
- Cause and Effect Diagram
- FMEA
- Process Mapping
- Hypothesis Testing
- ANOVA
- Correlation
- Linear Regression
- Theory of Constraints
- SMED (Single Minute Exchange of Dies)
- Total Productive Maintenance (TPM)
- Design for Six Sigma
- Quality Function Deployment
- DOE – Design of Experiments
- Control Charts
- Control Plan

A description of the above topics is beyond the scope of this brief book. Interested readers can find ready commercial references on all the topics. Some suggested references are provided in the References for Chapter 5.

Chapter 5 References

1. Agustiady, Tina and Badiru, A. B. (2013), **Sustainability: Utilizing Lean Six Sigma Techniques**, Taylor & Francis CRC Press, Boca Raton, FL, 2013.
2. Badiru, A. B. and Tina Kovach (2012), **Statistical Techniques for Project Control**, Taylor & Francis CRC Press, Boca Raton, FL, 2012.

3. Badiru, A. B.; Abi Badiru; Ade Badiru (2008), **Industrial Project Management: Concepts, Tools, and Techniques**, Taylor & Francis CRC Press, Boca Raton, FL, 2008.
4. Badiru, A. B. (2021), **Project Management Essentials: Analytics for Control**, Taylor & Francis CRC Press, Boca Raton, FL, 2021.
5. Badiru, A. B. (2019), **Project Management: Systems, Principles, and Applications**, Second Edition, Taylor & Francis CRC Press, Boca Raton, FL, 2019.
6. Badiru, Adedeji B. (2019), **Systems Engineering Models: Theory, Methods, and Applications,** Taylor & Francis/CRC Press, Boca Raton, FL, 2019.

CHAPTER 6

USING WBS FOR TIME MANAGEMENT

"The nucleus of a task is in splitting it in two"
– Adedeji Badiru

Work is best accomplished in smaller chunks of efforts that are organized hierarchically. The technique of Work Breakdown Structure (WBS) is commonly used for this purpose. It is a simple approach to representing the foundation over which a goal is developed and managed. WBS refers to the itemization of a project for planning, scheduling, and control purposes. WBS defines the end goal or scope of a project. The WBS diagram presents the inherent components of a project in a structured block diagram or interrelationship flow chart. WBS shows the relative hierarchies of parts (phases, segments, milestone, etc.) of the endeavor. The purpose of constructing a WBS is to analyze the elemental components of the project in detail. If a project is properly designed through the application of WBS at the project planning stage, it becomes easier to estimate time requirements for the components of the project. Project control is also enhanced by the ability to identify how the components link together. Tasks that are contained in the WBS collectively describe the overall project goal. A large project may be broken down into smaller sub-projects that may, in turn, be systematically broken down into task groups. As conveyed in the opening quote for this chapter, the essence of a task is found when the task is divided into its components. WBS permits the implementation of a "divide and conquer" concept for project control. This fits the purpose of the 8-by-3 paradigm introduced in this book.

Individual components in a WBS are referred to as WBS elements, and the hierarchy of each is designated by a Level identifier. Elements at the same level of subdivision are said to be of the same WBS level. Descending levels provide increasingly detailed definition of project tasks. The complexity of a project and the degree of control desired will determine the number of levels in the WBS. Each component is successively broken down into smaller details at lower levels. The process may continue until specific project activities (WBS elements) are reached. In effect, the structure of the WBS looks very much like an organizational chart. The 8-by-3 paradigm mimics a WBS-type breakdown of a 24-hour day.

A simple and familiar example of the application of the WBS structure is the purchase of a new car. In this case, "Car Purchase" is the final goal. Some of the lower-level objectives include "Get Finance," "Sell Old Car," "Trade-in Old Car," "Clean Old Car to get it ready for the market," "Consult with insurance agent," and "Do market research of latest car models." These can be organized into hierarchical levels to form a structure of how the eventual goal can be accomplished. The basic approach for preparing a WBS is as follows:

Level 1 WBS: This level contains only the final goal. For the purpose of implementing the 8-by-3 paradigm, this item should be identifiable directly as a personal need with respect to the prevailing environmental factors, such as home, work, family, and leisure.

Level 2 WBS: This level contains the major sub-sections of the goal. These sub-sections are usually identified by their contiguous locations or by their related purposes.

Level 3 WBS: This level of the WBS contains definable components of the level 2 sub-sections. In operational terms, this may be referred to as the finite details level of the end goal.

Subsequent levels of WBS may be constructed in more specific details depending on the span of control and flexibility desired. If a complete WBS becomes too crowded, separate WBS layouts may be drawn for the Level 2 components. In order to make a WBS for the 8-by-3 paradigm practical for an individual, the goals and objectives should consider the scope of effort, resource requirements, and feasibility of the endeavor. Sometimes, we tend to be over-ambitious with our undertakings with respect to time availability, time requirement, resource requirement, resource availability, and our own capability to deliver. Such a misjudgment of personal capability often spells doom and failure in getting things done.

The 8-by-3 paradigm is very amenable to personal customization for the user's specific situation and prevailing needs. Each person must determine where and how each block of time can be allocated. The key requirement is to have the self-discipline, fortitude, and personal dedication to stick with the time allotments. A popular Nigerian Yoruba saying provides the following guidance:

"You cannot use someone else's clock to
set your own work schedule."

You must map your own capability and personal references to the requirements of the job, with the eventual goal of getting the job done well and on time.

TBS: Time Breakdown Structure

"If it weren't for the last minute, nothing
would get done." - Rita Mae Brown

As humans, we love living on the edge of time. The opening quote above highlights the importance of last-minute execution of our task responsibilities. As illustrated in the hour-glass diagram below, the passage of time ticks and must be allocated efficiently from one stage of work to the next stage. In the same way that a work breakdown structure is developed, a time breakdown structure can also be developed for implementing the 8-by-3 paradigm of time management. Time management is the process of identifying specific actions to be performed to produce the deliverables of a project. The basic requirements are the following:

- Create a WBS structure that identifies time-based deliverables at the lowest level (e.g., work packages and due dates).
- Decomposed work packages into smaller timed activities (e.g., work duration start and end points).
- Use the smaller activities for estimating, scheduling, executing, monitoring, and controlling the flow of work and 8-by-3 time allocations.

The concept of SMART (Specific, Measurable, Aligned, Realistic, and Timed) is useful in accomplishing a time breakdown structure of projects as listed below:

Specific: Tasks in the breakdown structure must be specific.

Measurable: Tasks in the breakdown structure must be measurable.

Aligned: Tasks in the breakdown structure must be aligned and achievable within the overall project goal.

Realistic: Tasks in the breakdown structure must be realistic and relevant to the organization.

Timed: Tasks in the breakdown structure must have a time basis.

Crashing is the expediting or compression of activity duration. Crashing is done as a trade-off between a shorter task duration and a higher task cost. It must be determined whether the total cost savings realized from reducing the project duration is enough to justify the higher costs associated with reducing individual task durations. If there is a delay penalty associated with a project, it may be possible to reduce the total project cost even though crashing increases individual task costs.

If the cost savings on the delay penalty are higher than the incremental cost of reducing the project duration, then crashing is justified. Normal task duration refers to the time required to perform a task under normal circumstances. Crash task duration refers to the reduced time required to perform a task when additional resources are allocated to it.

If each activity is assigned a range of time and cost estimates, then several combinations of time and cost values will be associated with the overall project. Iterative procedures are used to determine the best time or cost combination for a project. Time-cost trade-off analysis may be conducted, for example, to determine the marginal cost of reducing the duration of the project by one time unit. Critical chain is the theory of constraints applied to project management specifically for managing and scheduling projects and controlling critical path activities. Constraint management is based on the principle that the performance of a system's constraint will determine the performance of the entire system. If a project's characteristic constraint is effectively managed, the overall project will be effectively managed. This is analogous to the belief that the worst performer of an organization will dictate the performance of the organization. Similarly, the weakest link in a chain determines the strength of the chain. Because overall operation is essentially a series of linkages of activities, one break in the linkage determines a break of the overall operation. That is, it takes only one negative to negate a series of positives. That is, $(+)(+)(+)(+)(+)(+)(-) = (-)$. Looking at this from a production point of view, a bottleneck operation will determine the throughput of an overall production system. From a group operation point of view, the last passenger on a complimentary shuttle bus determines the departure time of the bus. What all these examples mean in the context of project scheduling is that our focus should be on the critical activities in the project network diagram. For the purpose of managing time breakdown of tasks that make up a project, you need to recognize the following constraints:

- Policy-based restrictions on activity time splitting
- Physical or technical limitations on activity time splitting
- Project environment limitations on activity time splitting

Each constraint type impacts the project differently. For project scheduling purposes, the critical chain is used to generate several alterations to the traditional network of project activities. All individual activity slacks or buffers become the overall project buffer. Each team member, responsible for his or her component of the activity network, creates a duration estimate free from any padding. The typical approach is to estimate time based on a 50% probability of success. All activities on the critical chain (path) and feeder chains (non-critical chains in the network) then are linked with minimal time padding. The project buffer now is aggregated and some proportion of the saved time is added to the project. Even adding 50% of the saved time significantly reduces the overall project schedule while requiring team members to be concerned less with activity padding and more with task completion. Even if the project team members miss their delivery date 50% of the time, the overall effect on the project's duration is minimized because of the downstream aggregated buffer.

If the concept of time breakdown structure presented in this chapter is followed, you can use the critical chain approach for tasks that are not on the critical chain. Accordingly, all feeder path activities are reduced by the same order of magnitude and a feeder buffer is constructed for the overall non-critical chain of activities. It should be noted that critical chain distinguishes between its use of buffer and the traditional project network use of project slack. Project slack is a function of the overall completed activity network. In other words, a slack is an outcome of the task dependencies, whereas critical chain buffer is used for planning and it is based on a logical redesign of each activity. The lesson conveyed in this chapter is that instead of lumping activity times into a big block, the elements that make up the block should be recognized and identified for the purpose of a better management practice along the line of using the 8-by-3 paradigm.

CHAPTER 7

USING CBS FOR TIME MANAGEMENT

"Where time goes, cost follows."
– Adedeji Badiru

Cost breakdown structure (CBS), which is a derivative of Work Breakdown Structure (WBS), can help identify potential avenues for saving not only money, but also saving time. Thus, CBS can be effective for time management. Just as in the corporate environment, cost tracking is an important aspect of personal time management. Understanding how cost breakdowns affect an overall goal makes it easier to manage how personal time is allocated. This is directly relevant for implementing the 8-by-3 paradigm. Money, as an object of cost, is a concern for everyone. Thus, understanding some basic concepts of cost can lead to saving money and, consequently, time. The decision of rent, lease, or buy, which more and more consumers face frequently, has its basis in an understanding of cost breakdowns. Likewise, the decision of whether to do it yourself (DIY) or hire an expert is faced by homeowners again and again. These decision scenarios have direct time management implications. For example, if you choose to use DIY to undertake a repair in your home, you need to consider the following:

- How much the repair man will cost?
- How long will it take the repair man?
- Will you have to provide some "hang-around-and-watch" time to monitor the repair man?
- If you choose to do it yourself (DIY), do you have the time?
- If after several hours of DIY effort, you still end up hiring a professional to do the job well, the personal time spent is lost and cannot be recovered.
- If you do commit your personal time to do the repair, how will you save how much your personal time is worth, in terms of opportunity cost of your not being at work earning a salary?
- Is the DIY time that you allocate for the repair detracting you away from other priorities?
- Do you have sufficient skills for the DIY project to avoid a costly rework?

These considerations influence the decision of how you allocate your time and cost, within the context of the 8-by-3 paradigm. The term "cost management" refers to the functions required to maintain effective monetary control of your endeavors. Within a given scope of analysis, there may be a combination of different types of cost aspects to consider. These cost aspects include the ones explained below:

Actual cost of work performed: the cost actually incurred and recorded in accomplishing the work performed within a given period of time.

Applied Direct Cost: the amounts recognized in the time period associated with the consumption of labor, material, and other direct resources, without regard to the date of commitment or the date of payment. These amounts are charged to the work-in-process (WIP) when resources are actually consumed, material resources are withdrawn from inventory for use, or material resources are received and scheduled for use within the planning horizon.

Budgeted cost for work performed: the sum of the budgets for completed work plus the appropriate portion of the budgets for the level of effort and apportioned effort. Apportioned effort is effort that, by itself, is not readily divisible into short-span work packages but is related in direct proportion to the measured effort.

Budgeted cost for work scheduled: the sum of budgets for all work packages and planning packages scheduled to be accomplished (including work in process) plus the amount of level of effort and apportioned effort scheduled to be accomplished within a given period of time.

Direct cost: cost that is directly associated with actual operations of a project. Typical sources of direct costs are direct material costs and direct labor costs. Direct costs are those that can be reasonably measured and allocated to a specific component of a project.

Economies of Scale: a reduction of the relative weight of the fixed cost in the total cost by increasing output quantity. This helps to reduce the final unit cost of an undertaking. Economies of scale are often simply referred to as the savings due to mass production.

Estimated cost at completion: the actual direct costs, plus indirect costs that can be allocated to the project, plus estimated costs (direct and indirect) for the authorized work remaining.

First cost: the total initial investment required to initiate a project or the total initial cost of the equipment needed to start the project.

Fixed cost: a cost incurred irrespective of the level of operation of a project. Fixed costs do not vary in proportion to the quantity of output. Examples of costs that make up the fixed cost of a project are administrative expenses, certain types of taxes, insurance cost, depreciation cost, and debt-servicing cost. These costs usually do not vary in proportion to the quantity of output.

Incremental cost: the additional cost of changing the production output from one level to another. Incremental costs are normally variable costs.

Indirect cost: a cost that is indirectly associated with project operations. Indirect costs are those that are difficult to assign to specific components of a project. An example of an indirect cost is the cost of computer hardware and software needed to manage project operations. Indirect costs are usually calculated as a percentage of a component of direct costs. For example, the indirect costs may be computed as 10% of direct labor costs.

Life-cycle cost: the sum of all costs, recurring and nonrecurring, associated with a project during its entire life cycle. Individuals typically don't recognize the life-cycle costs of their household projects. For example, a DIY project may cost a home owner less initially upfront, but may have recurring later costs not previously anticipated or estimated by the homeowner. These costs may include cost of repair, cost of redo, or cost of calling in an expert repair man in an emergency.

Maintenance cost: a cost that occurs intermittently or periodically and is used for the purpose of keeping project equipment or resources in good operating condition.

Marginal cost: the additional cost of increasing production output by one additional unit. The marginal cost is equal to the slope of the total cost curve or line at the current operating level.

Operating cost: a recurring cost needed to keep a project in operation during its life cycle. Operating costs may consist of such items as labor cost, material cost, and energy cost.

Opportunity cost: the cost of forgoing the opportunity to invest in a venture that would have produced an economic advantage. Opportunity costs are usually incurred due to limited resources that make it impossible to take advantage of all investment opportunities. This is often defined as the cost of the best rejected opportunity. Opportunity costs can also be incurred due to a missed opportunity rather than due to an intentional rejection. In many cases, opportunity costs are hidden or implied because they typically relate to future events that cannot be accurately predicted.

Overhead cost: a cost incurred for activities performed in support of the operations of a project. The activities that generate overhead costs support the project efforts rather than contribute directly to the project goal. The handling of overhead costs varies widely from company to company. Typical overhead items are electric power cost, insurance premiums, cost of security, and inventory carrying cost.

Standard cost: a cost that represents the normal or expected cost of a unit of the output of an operation. Standard costs are established in advance. They are developed as a composite of several elemental costs, such as direct labor cost per unit, material cost per unit, and allowable overhead charge per unit.

Sunk cost: This is a cost that occurred in the past and cannot be recovered under the present scenario. Sunk costs should have no bearing on the prevailing economic analysis and project decisions. Ignoring sunk costs is always a difficult task for individuals. For example, if $50,000 was spent four years ago to buy a piece of equipment, a decision on whether or not to replace the equipment now should not consider that initial cost. But sentiments may make it difficult to ignore so much money invested upfront. Similarly, an individual making a decision on selling a personal automobile would typically try to relate the asking price to what was paid for the automobile when it was acquired. This is untenable under the concept of sunk costs.

Total cost: the sum of all the variable and fixed costs associated with a project.

Variable cost: a cost that varies in direct proportion to the level of operation or quantity of output. For example, the costs of material and labor required to make an item are categorized as variable costs since they vary with changes in the level of output.

Cost estimation and budgeting help establish a strategy for allocating resources to endeavors. There are three major categories of cost estimation for budgeting based on the desired level of accuracy:

1. Order-of-magnitude estimates
2. Preliminary cost estimates
3. Detailed cost estimates

Order-of-magnitude cost estimates are usually gross estimates based on the experience and judgment of the estimator. They are sometimes called "ballpark" figures. These estimates are typically made without a formal evaluation of the details involved in the project. Order-of-magnitude estimates can range, in terms of accuracy, from -50% to +50% of the actual cost. Preliminary cost estimates are also gross estimates, but with a higher level of accuracy. In developing preliminary cost estimates, more attention is paid to some selected details of the project. An example of a preliminary cost estimate is the estimation of expected labor cost. Preliminary estimates are useful for evaluating project alternatives before final commitments are made. The level of accuracy associated with preliminary estimates can ranges from -20% to +20% of the actual cost. Detailed cost estimates are developed after careful consideration is given to all the major details of a project. Considerable time is typically needed to obtain detailed cost estimates. Because of the amount of time and effort needed to develop detailed cost estimates, the estimates are usually developed after there is a firm commitment that the project will happen. Detailed cost estimates are also important for evaluating actual cost performance during the project. The level of accuracy associated with detailed estimates normally range from -5% to +5% of the actual cost. There are two basic approaches to generating cost estimates. The first one is a variant approach, in which cost estimates are based on variations of previous cost records. The other approach is the generative cost estimation, in which cost estimates are developed from scratch without taking previous cost records into consideration.

Flavors of Cost Estimates

Cost estimates can fall in one of the following three categories:

- Optimistic cost estimate
- Most likely cost estimate
- Pessimistic cost estimate

In a corporate process, the most likely estimated cost is guessed to be four times as likely to occur as either the optimistic or pessimistic times. Thus, the average or expected cost is calculated as the optimistic estimate plus four times the most likely estimate plus the pessimistic estimate, all divided by six. This average calculation provides a reasonable guidance of what an endeavor can cost. Having a good estimate for cost expectations can guide the allocation of time to the tasks that have to be done within each block of 8-by-3 paradigm. We will get a better handle on cost and time management if we can determine where costs are allocated. Where cost goes, time follows and vice versa. A Pareto Chart is a simple tool for analyzing cost and time distribution. The chart can help to view the causes of a problem in the order of severity from the largest to the smallest. The Pareto principle of 80-20 distribution rule is commonly expressed in the operational statements below:

- 20% of your activities consume 80% of your cost.
- 20% of your project takes up 80% of your project time.

This states that, for many items, about 80% of the value comes from 20% of the items. This is often stated as the rule of the "vital few" and the "trivial many." For the purpose of implementing the 8-by-3 paradigm, activities may be put into Pareto categories for a more efficient control of the time and cost associated with the activities. The Pareto distribution can be extended to the ABC analysis, in which items are put into A, B, and C categories having different levels of significance. The categories are handled and controlled differently based on their differing levels of significance. In the ABC distribution, the following applies:

- The 'A' items are very important. These require the greatest attention.
- The B' items are important. These require moderate attention.
- The 'C' items are marginally important. These require less attention.

There are no fixed cut-off points for each category. Different percentage levels can be applied based on the prevailing circumstance and the needs of the user. Some examples are presented below:

'A' items make up 20% of the project, but accounts for 70% of the total project time.

'B' items make up 30% of the project, accounts for 25% of the total project time.

'C' items make up 50% of the project, but accounts for 5% of the total project time.

Time and cost are often linked. Like they say, "time is money." If we can manage our time effectively, we can have a better control of our cost. As a project progresses, costs can be monitored and evaluated to identify areas of unacceptable cost performance. We can develop real or hypothetical plot of cost versus time for the planned cost and the actual cost. The plot permits a quick identification of when cost overruns occur in a project life cycle. In accordance with the 8-by-3 paradigm of time management, monitoring cost provides an avenue for a more effective management of time.

CHAPTER 8

OVERCOMING TIME ROBBERS

"Preemption of time robbers is better than
correction of time robbers."
– Adedeji Badiru

Time robbers are non-value-adding activities that creep into our schedules. Many times, we engage time robbers deliberately and consciously, even though we may not immediately realize their adverse impacts on our overall time efficiency. Sometimes, time robbers encroach into our schedules "uninvited." The 8-by-3 paradigm can help mitigate the adverse effects of both conscious and sub-conscious time robbers. This can be accomplished through the explicit technique of activity scheduling, which allocates a time block for each activity. By explicit scheduling of activities, time robbers can be more easily identified upfront and preempted. If a time robber is allowed to encroach and entrench itself into our schedule, it may be difficult to eradicate later on. For this reason, the tenet offered by the chapter-opening quote above is relevant for the implementation of the 8-by-3 paradigm of time management.

Activity sequencing is the time-phased scheduling of activities subject to precedence relationships, time constraints, and resource limitations to accomplish specific objectives. The critical path method (CPM) is a network technique that presents a visual representation of activity sequencing. CPM charts are excellent visual communication tools for conveying project scope, requirements, and lines of responsibility. A project consists of activities that are mapped against a timeline. Projects usually involve one-time endeavors that may not necessarily be duplicated in identical circumstances. In some cases, it may be possible to duplicate the concepts of the whole project or a portion of it in subsequent executions of the project. Several techniques are available for planning, scheduling, and controlling projects. The available scheduling techniques and solution approaches can be categorized as follows:

- Unconstrained resources
  - Critical path analysis
  - Time-cost trade-off problem
- Constrained resources
  - Rule-of-thump techniques
  - Mathematical techniques

Project schedules may be complex, unpredictable, and dynamic. Complexity may be due to interdependencies of activities, multiple resource requirements, multiple concurrent events, multiple conflicting objectives, technical constraints, and schedule conflicts. Unpredictability may be due to equipment breakdowns, raw material inconsistency (delivery and quality), operator performance, worker absenteeism, and unforeseen events. Dynamism may be due to resource variability, changes in scope of work, and resource substitutions.

Predictive scheduling is a proactive scheduling approach that attempts to anticipate the potential causes of schedule problems. These problems are corrected by contingency plans. Reactive scheduling is a scheduling approach that reacts to problems that develop during project execution. The premise of the 8-by-3 paradigm is to preempt reactive scheduling of activities. If activities are scheduled to take place during their assigned blocks of time, the need for reactive and corrective reshuffling of activities will be minimized.

Network planning is sometimes referred to as activity planning. This involves the identification of the relevant activities making up a project.

The required activities and their precedence relationships are determined. Precedence requirements may be determined on the basis of the following:

1. Technical limitations
2. Procedural requirements
3. Imposed constraints

Technical precedence requirements are caused by the technical relationships among activities in a project. For example, in the conventional construction of a building, walls must be erected before the roof can be installed. Procedural precedence requirements are determined by policies and procedures. Such policies and procedures are often subjective without a sound justification. Imposed precedence requirements can be classified as resource-imposed, scenario-imposed, or environment-imposed. For example, resource shortages may require that one task be scheduled before another. The current status of a project (e.g., percent completion) may determine that one activity be performed before another. The environment of a project, for example, weather changes or the effects of concurrent projects, may determine the precedence relationships of the activities in a project. Based on these precedence relationships, the activities in the project are sequenced pictorially to form a project network diagram. Time, cost, and resource requirement estimates are developed for each activity during the network planning phase. The estimates may be based on personal preference, historical records, time standards, forecasting, regression functions, or other data-based models.

Network scheduling is performed by using forward-pass and backward-pass calculations. These calculations give the earliest and latest starting and finishing times for each activity. The amount of slack associated with each activity is also determined during the calculation process. The activity path with the minimum slack in the network is used to determine the critical activities. This path also determines the duration of the project. Resource allocation, and time-cost trade-offs are other functions performed during network scheduling. The critical activities, thus determined, represent where the project should focus its attention. These high-priority activities fit the concept and procedures of the 8-by-3 paradigm of time management. Network control involves tracking the progress of a project on the basis of the network schedule and taking corrective actions when needed. An evaluation of actual performance versus expected performance determines deficiencies in the project progress. The advantages of activity sequencing for project control include the following:

- Advantages for communication
  i.   Clarification of objectives
  ii. Establishment of the specifications for project performance
  iii. Provision of a starting point for more detailed task analysis
  iv. Representation of a documentation of the project plan
  v.   Pictorial representation of the project scope

- Advantages for control
  vi.   Presentation of a measure for evaluating project performance
  vii. Help in determining what corrective actions are needed
  viii. Presentation of a clear message of what is expected
  ix.   Encouragement for follow up projects

- Advantages for team interaction
  x.   A mechanism for a quick introduction to the project
  xi.   Specification of functional interfaces of the project
  xii. Facilitation of teamwork

For the purpose of a practical implementation of the 8-by-3 paradigm, the blocks really don't have to be equal in duration or finitely bounded. Depending on each person's needs, the block may be sequenced, with each block filled with activity scheduling fitting the user's specific needs. For example, for those working permanent night duties, such as doctors, nurses, and security personnel, it may be necessary to customize the blocks to their specific and unique work situations.

Signatures create more bottlenecks in the corporate world than anything else of the same time magnitude. The act of signing a document, itself, does not consume much time, but the wait time to obtain a high-level signature can be problematic in the overall activity scheduling process. Also, an erroneous preparation of a document to be signed can be a source of a lengthy delay. For example re-doing and re-signing a document can consume a lot of time that is not planned or scheduled into the work process. It is essential to be prudent upfront to preempt rework and time delays.

When scheduling multiple activities over several days, don't try to do too much all at the same time. Being overloaded can lead to inefficient use of time. Rather, it is expedient to attempt to accomplish at least one major task each day. Some common examples are:

- Complete income tax paperwork
- Pay bills
- Take car for service
- Exercise
- Do laundry
- Do auto registration
- Do grocery shopping
- Mow the lawn
- Reorganize file cabinet
- Send out party invitation cards

If an item is not scheduled, it may not get done. By scheduling and focusing on major activity completions one at a time, one item will not get in the way of another, thereby preserving the integrity of the 8-by-3 paradigm.

CHAPTER 9

WORK RATE ANALYSIS FOR TIME MANAGEMENT

"You must know where your cost is buried."
– Adedeji Badiru

"I like work. It fascinates me. I can sit and look at it for hours." - Jerome K Jerome (Comedian). This quote begs the question: "What is the work rate of looking at work for hours?" Work rate measurement is a simple technique of measuring and assessing how quickly (or slowly) work is accomplished. When team members work concurrently at different work rates, the amount of work accomplished by each may be computed by work rate calculations. The general relationship between work, work rate and time is that work is equal to the work rate multiplied by the work duration. Work is the amount of actual output accomplished. This is expressed in appropriate units, such as miles of road completed, lines of computer codes typed, gallons of oil spill cleaned, units of widgets produced, surface area painted, or number of donuts made. Work rate per unit time is the rate at which the assigned work is accomplished. Duration is how long it times to accomplish the work. Relative cost, time, and quality measurements are essential for work rate time measurement. However, "quickly" does not have to sacrifice efficiency, effectiveness, integrity, and consistency.

It is assumed that work rates remain constant for the duration of the work being analyzed. Work is defined as a physical measure of accomplishment with a uniform density (i.e., homogeneous). For example, one-square-footage of construction may be said to be homogeneous if one-square-footage is as complex and desirable as any other square footage. Hamburger production is homogenous if the production process is uniform and consistent, thereby making all hamburgers equally satisfying in taste, value, cost, weight, and so on. Similarly, cleaning one gallon of oil spill is as good as cleaning any other gallon of oil spill within the same work environment. The production of one unit of a product is identical to the production of any other unit of the production of any other unit of the same product. If a uniform work density can be assumed for the particular work being analyzed, then the relationship is defined as one whole unit, and the following relationship will be applicable for the case of a single person performing the work: Work rate multiplied by the work duration equals one whole unit of work.

For example, if a construction worker can build one block in thirty minutes, then his work rate is 1/30 of a block per minute. If the magnitude of the denominator of the work rate is greater than the magnitude of the work duration, then only a fraction of the required work will be performed. The information about the proportion of work completed is useful for work planning, time allotment, and productivity measurement purposes. In the case of many people performing the work simultaneously as a team, the work relationship is expanded by summation to account for the group output relative to individual outputs. The examples that follow illustrate work rate calculations.

Suppose Person 1, working alone, can complete a job in 50 hours. After Person 1 has been working on the job for 10 hours, Person 2 was assigned to help Person 1 in completing the job. Both workers, working together, finished the remaining work in 15 hours. It is desired to determine the work rate of Person 2. The amount of work to be done is 1.0 whole unit. The work rate of Person 1 is 1/50 of work per unit time. Therefore, the amount of work completed by Person 1 in the 10 days he or she worked alone is $(1/50)(10) = 1/5$ of the required work. This may also be expressed in terms of percent completion. The remaining work to be done is 4/5 of the total work. The two workers working together for 15 hours produce the following result: 15/50 +15(work rate of Person 2) = 45, which yields1/30 for the work rate of Person 2. This means that Person 2, working alone, could perform the job in 30 hours. In this example, it is assumed that both workers produce identical quality of work. If quality levels are not identical for multiple workers, then the work rates may be adjusted to account for the different quality levels or a quality factor may be introduced into the analysis. The relative costs of the different workers needed to perform the required work may be incorporated into the analysis for a cost-based assessment.

As another example, suppose the work rate of Person 1 is such that he can perform a certain task in 30 hours. It is desired to add Person 2 to the task so that the completion time of the task could be reduced. The work rate of Person 2 is such that he can perform the same task alone in 22 hours. If Person 1 has already worked 12 hours on the task before Person 2 comes in, we want to find the completion time of the task. It is assumed that Person 1 starts the task at time 0. The amount of work to be done is 1.0 whole unit (i.e., the full task). The work rate of Person 1 is 1/30 of the task per unit time and the work rate of Person 2 is 1/22 of the task per unit time. The amount of work completed by Person 1 in the 12 hours he or she worked alone is (1/30)(12)=2/5 (or 40%) of the required work. Therefore, the remaining work to be done is 2/5 (or 60%) of the full task. Now, we let T be the time for which both people work together. Then, the two people working together to complete the task means that T/30+T/22=3/5, which yields T = 7.62 hours. Consequently, the completion time of the task is 12 + 7.62 = 19.62 hours. It is assumed that both workers produce identical quality of work and that the respective work rates remain consistent. An appreciation of the respective work rates is important in fitting activities into specific time blocks within the 8-by-3 paradigm.

CHAPTER 10

GETTING ORGANIZED FOR TIME MANAGEMENT

"To get things done promptly, organize,
organize, and organize again."
– Adedeji Badiru

"Tomorrow belongs to those who prepare for it today" (African Proverb). This proverb suggests that to do well tomorrow, we must prepare the path today. This means that being organized today will pave the way for a successful execution of tasks tomorrow. Being organized is a key requirement for managing time. For the 8-by-3 paradigm to be effective for you, you must be well organized to make proper allocations of tasks across the blocks of time. In the corporate environment, there are formal tools and techniques for organizing work. Those same techniques can be adopted for personal organization. One simple, but rigorous, approach for organizing work is the Japanese technique of 5s, which stipulates workplace discipline through a series of words starting with the letter "s." When five s-words are used, we have "5s" and when six words are used, we have "6s." The words are explained below:

1. Seiri (Sort): This means to distinguish between what is needed and not needed and remove the latter. The tools and materials in the workplace are sorted out. The unwanted tools and materials are placed in the Red Tag area, which is used for identifying, tagging, removing, and disposing of items that are not needed in the work area. It applied to the kitchen area in a home, it will mean removing from the kitchen all items not immediately needed in a typical day in the kitchen.

2. Seiton (Stabilize): This means to enforce a place for everything and everything in its place. The workplace is organized by labeling. The machines and tools are labeled with their names and all the sufficient data required. A sketch with exact scale of the work floor is drawn with grids. This helps in achieving a better flow of work and an easy access to all tools and machines.

3. Seison (Shine): This means to clean up the workplace and look for ways to keep it clean. Periodic cleaning and maintenance of the workplace and machines are done. The wastes are placed in a separate area. The recyclable and other wastes are separately placed in separate containers. This makes it easy to know where every component is placed. The clean look of the workplace helps in a better organization and increases the flow of work.

4. Seiketsu (Standardize): This means to maintain and monitor adherence to the first three s's. This process helps to standardize work. The work of each person is clearly defined. The suitable person is chosen for a particular work. People in the workplace should know who is responsible for what. The scheduling is standardized. Time is maintained for every work that is to be done. A set of rules is created to maintain the first 3s's. This helps in improving efficiency of the workplace.

5. Shitsuke (Sustain): This means to follow the rules to keep the workplace 5s-compliant to "maintain the gain." Once the previous 4s's are implemented some rules are developed for sustaining the other s's.

6. Safety: This refers to eliminating hazards in the work environment. The sixth "s" is added so that focus could be directed at safety within all improvement efforts. This is particularly essential in high-risk and accident-prone environments. This sixth extension is

often debated as a separate entity because safety should be implicit in everything we do. Besides, the Japanese word for Safety is "Anzen," which does not follow the "s" rhythm. Going further out on a limb, some practitioners even include additional levels of "s." So, we could have 8s with the addition of Security and Satisfaction.

7. Security: This could involve job security, personal security, mitigation of risk, capital security, intellectual security, property security, information security, asset security, equity security, product brand security, and so on.
8. Satisfaction: This could include personal satisfaction, employee satisfaction, morale, job satisfaction, sense of belonging, and so on.

If 5s is practiced with the seriousness of a corporate entity, a better management of time can be achieved. There is a lot of waste in our normal personal day-to-day activities. These wastes consume time in terms of tracking, storing, and maintaining. A waste is anything other than the minimum amount of equipment, materials, raw materials, parts, and storage space, which are definitely essential in adding value to work in progress. For example, in a kitchen, maintaining two sets of pots in the immediate vicinity of the stove constitutes a waste, which ultimately translates to time inefficiency.

In a corporate setting, the eight deadly wastes are identified as over production, product defects, inventory, excess process, transportation, excess motion, waiting, and under-utilizing resources (e.g., human resources). The same waste assessment can be done for the home environment, thereby identifying wasted efforts that lead to inefficient use of time. In summary, to save time, do the following:

- Things that are frequently used should be placed closer to the work bench.
- Things that are occasionally used should be located in the distant vicinity of the work site.
- Things that are rarely used should be placed in storage and out of the way.

The practice of the 5s technique complements the time blocking approach of the 8-by-3 paradigm.

CHAPTER 11

DEJI SYSTEMS MODEL FOR TIME MANAGEMENT

"A systems view of the world is what keeps the
wheel of performance well oiled."
– Adedeji Badiru

"A stitch in time saves nine." (An English Proverb). This Chapter Eleven arrives at the eleventh hour. Effective time management is based on a systems view of everything we do within whatever time we have. This chapter's opening quote conveys that a timely effort will preempt more later on, which is the premise of the 8 by3 paradigm. Conservation of time is the best way to save time. The tips below are offered as a guide to readers. They can be expanded to fit each person's needs and specific situations. The premise of each tip is that time can be saved by adopting time-conscious strategies at home, work, and leisure. The simple fact is that things that are done or not done have time implications somewhere down the line. If these time robbers can be preempted or averted in advance, we can avoid time-consuming corrections, reactions, or modifications later on. Issues that appear to be non-time-involved upfront always turn out to have underlying time implications when viewed in the context of full ramifications. In other words, everything has a time basis in the final analysis. Below are my own original tips that I offer to the potential adopters of the 8-by-3 paradigm:

- Accept the existence of differences in others; it saves you time in dealing with them.
- Acquire new skills so that you can succeed in new environments; this costs less time.
- Anticipate obstacles; it takes less time to preempt than to fight and defeat.
- Anticipate problems and preempt them; time, thus saved, can be used for other purposes.
- Apologize promptly when needed; this saves time later on.
- Ask questions, not to criticize, but to learn more about the problem scenario.
- Assess your own talents and interests and leverage them to craft your goals and objectives.
- At work, home, or in the public, respect yourself so that others may respect you.
- At work, home, or play, follow through on commitments to create a reputation of reliability.
- Avoid loathsome disposition; it reflects back onto yourself.
- Avoid personal vendetta; it only chews up your time.
- Avoid punitive reactions; it costs time to be vengeful.
- Avoid retaliation just for the sake of getting even; there is no value in vengeance.
- Avoid silo-typical approach to your work and capability; getting help from others saves time.
- Avoid pessimism; it only sees the cloudy part of the day.
- Balance the need for additional information with the expediency of moving forward to action.
- Be a dependable steward of organizational resources; saving resources saves time.
- Be a pleasure to work with; it will take you less time to seek collaboration.
- Be approachable; intimidation will cost you more time when trying to seal a deal.

- Be consistent in your actions and utterances; dilly-dallying costs time.
- Be fair and consistent; fairness cost less time.
- Be happy with yourself, knowing that you have managed your time effectively.
- Be honest and trustworthy; this will avoid you having to spend time defending yourself.
- Be open and receptive to others' ideas; it costs less time to commend than to fight the ideas.
- Be open to new ideas; you may learn time-saving tricks.
- Be optimistic while being cognizant of potential pitfalls.
- Be reliable and dependable; it will save you time in your interactions with others.
- Be SMART with your engagements (Specific, Measurable, Achievable, Realistic, Timed).
- Be tolerant of the views of others; there is a gem in everyone.
- Be willing to learn from your subordinates; you don't have all the answers.
- Challenge yourself and thrive as you overcome the pain of tribulations.
- Communicate to inspire others; they may reciprocate with time-saving kindness.
- Compliment often; it doesn't cost time or money.
- Conserve time; it is the basis for all endeavors.
- Coordinate responsibilities to facilitate expeditious completion of projects.
- Delegate as needed so that you can direct your time toward more critical needs.
- Demonstrate a positive attitude regardless of the prevailing challenges.
- Demonstrate professionalism in all you do.
- Develop a passion for self-advancement; time efficiency in around the corner.
- Develop a vision and share it with others; they will be there to assist you.
- Develop an inclusive embrace for co-workers; they will accept you and save you time.

- Develop and sustain a "can-do" attitude to all challenges; giving up early is the door of failure.
- Discpline yourself when you have erred; this avoids having someone else do it.
- Do actual work to pass the time; do not whine away the time with complaints about work.
- Do it and forget it, so that you may move on to spending your time on other things.
- Do the right thing when no one is watching; personal gratification is as good as public accolades.
- Do the right thing the first time, so that you won't have to spend time doing it over again.
- Do things fast; timely execution of tasks creates more time for the next achievement.
- Do now, what you need to do. There is never a better time to do it.
- Do what you must before being forced to do it; being proactive saves time.
- Don't be a hard-baller; give-and-take takes the day in the long run.
- Don't be a procrastinator extraordinaire. Do it now, if you are going to do it at all.
- Don't blame others for your own failings; acceptance is the first order of getting better.
- Don't despair when a failure occurs; there is always a way to make amendments.
- Don't dilly-dally on simple decisions that have no business being delayed.
- Don't do Winter projects in the Summer and don't do Summer project in the Winter; it will cost you more time to flip-flop projects.
- Don't let minor problems fester into bigger problems, which will cost you more time.
- Don't multitask incompatible tasks; decoupling overlapped tasks costs more time.
- Don't put off what can be done and dismissed now.
- Don't try to do too much; being overstretched will erode your productivity.

- Don't try to do too many things at once; it leads to costly cut-corner temptations.
- Don't while away your time by engaging in destructive whining.
- Embrace the notion that preemption is better than correction.
- Embrace, promote, and leverage change; it is good for keeping things lively.
- Evaluate alternatives and new perspectives; new discoveries may be found.
- Exhibit empathy and compassion for others; you may need same from them some day.
- Exhibit respect for others; it will save you time when they reciprocate.
- Focus on a positive outcome even if the path is paved with difficulties.
- Focus on the end result; it provides "light-at-the-end-of-the-tunnel" motivation.
- Have respect for time; it is the basis for all your accomplishments.
- Identify and focus on the most significant priorities.
- Imagine possibilities and opportunities; that is where success resides.
- In the work place, whether you are the boss or the underling, contribute to the work environment in a way that makes everyone feel valued.
- Interact with others positively; remember the Biblical exhortation of "Do unto others as you would have others do unto you."
- Keep priorities few and manageable; over-ambition paves the way for disappointment.
- Keep things simple; it takes less time to do simple things.
- Know that life-long learning leads to a longer life.
- Know that proactive ethical standards avoid time-consuming corrective actions later on.
- Know that a shared vision is better than a solo vision.
- Know that what is worth doing at all is worth doing now (or soon).
- Lead by example always; be prepared to follow as needed.
- Leverage your personal knowledge and experience in your decision-making processes.

- Link the current situation to guide future expectations and time management.
- Listen and learn; you cannot learn while talking.
- Listen well the first time; having to be told again will cost you time.
- Live by optimism; it sees only the rays of sunshine of the day and hope for the future.
- Maintain a vibrant perspective; stagnancy gets no one no where.
- Maintain upright personal behavior to enhance performance.
- Manage your emotions as tightly as you manage your time.
- Minimize travel in bad weather; getting stuck will cost you time.
- Monitor, track, and re-evaluate the execution of your plans.
- Preserve time; it is the foundation for success.
- Put organizational needs above personal gains; a successful organization is your success.
- Put others at ease; you gain more by not scaring people off.
- Put principles above personality in work relationships; being principled saves time.
- Recognize and acknowledge the contributions of others.
- Recognize internal and external factors influencing your actions.
- Recognize problems before they take root.
- Recognize that everything is time-sensitive; putting something off costs more time later.
- Recognize that foresight enhances hindsight.
- Recognize that later is not necessarily better when executing tasks.
- Recognize that no situation is permanent (except death); "up" can become "down" and vice versa.
- Recognize that the "do-nothing" alternative is always an option; it may be less time costly.
- Respond with calmness and composure; an agitated reaction clouds good judgment.
- Retire to bed early; most bad things happen at night.
- Reward yourself when you have earned it; this provides a lasting motivation.
- Schedule your daytime well; so that you won't have to roam the night.

- Seek cooperation explicitly from those you work with.
- Seek new innovative ways to improve things.
- Solve problems from an integrative perspective; integration saves time.
- Stand behind your decisions; a firm stand costs less time.
- Stand by those who stand by you.
- Stick to your budget; budget consistency requires less time to manage.
- Strive to do the right thing always; the right thing is right for saving time.
- Support others so that they may support you.
- Swallow your pride when necessary; it will cost you less time to make amendments.
- Take responsibility for your own actions.
- Task yourself to be a positive role model always.
- Think of consequences before embarking on time costly actions.
- Note that time management requires the same level of dedication and seriousness that we apply to our money management.
- Train others to have the skills to pick up slacks that may help lessen your own load.
- Train others to help you with your own objectives.
- Use available data to develop accurate and relevant decision analysis.
- Use mistakes as learning opportunities to leverage in moving on to the next accomplishment.
- Use personal leadership to exercise self-management and time control.
- Use past experience to direct future goal setting.
- Use cold and wet days for indoor chores and use warm and dry days for outdoor chores.
- View the world as a system of inter-connected needs and requirements.
- Walk when you can; your health is worth the walk.
- Why not do now, what you are going to do eventually?

"Early to bed, early to rise is the secret of time management
to get more done each day." – Adedeji Badiru

Problem Preemption Tips to Save Time

On the road:

- Think safety first and foremost.
- Note that haste makes waste in the end.
- Anticipate the stupid acts of other drivers.
- Be mindful that if it is stupidly possible, some driver will do it.
- Be defensive-minded around other drivers.
- Act as if you are the other drivers' keeper.
- Be a responsible shared-road user.
- Avoid reckless driving so that road problems will avoid you.
- Know that your destination is not running away; why do you have to chase it?
- Know that easy does it; hard-nosed driving will lead to a hard break.
- Don't drink and drive; the 8-by-3 model allocates time for each task.
- Don't text and drive; communication never expires, it will still be there.
- Predetermine a safe route to travel; avoid last-minute brash moves.
- Eat before you drive; avoid hunger-induced food fidgeting on the steering wheel.
- Recognize that foot and bike traffic is a part of the overall traffic system.
- If you see a car in traffic with banged up bumper, take note and avoid the car. The driver may have a record of involvement in traffic mishaps and may not care about tangling with your vehicle. Remember the broken window syndrome.

At home:

- Put tools where they belong so that time is saved in retrieving them later.
- Maintain good housekeeping; it makes it easier and faster to sort things out.
- Organize assets; this helps to find things when needed, thus saving time.

- Save leftovers for later use; this saves time from preparing fresh dishes too often.
- Clean as you go; accumulated dirt takes more time to clean at once.
- Don't lounge around the basement all day on a good-weather day. Get out and use the bright daylight to clean your garage, clean roof gutters, or mow the lawn.
- Do at night, what you don't need daylight to do.
- Do at daylight, what you need outside daylight to do.
- Keep yourself healthy. It is through good health that you can spend time on your tasks.
- Avoid time-robbing unhealthy habits:
  - Don't smoke.
  - Don't drink excessively.
  - Don't drink and drive. It will eventually rob you of your time.
  - Don't sacrifice your sleep. Adequate sleep rejuvenates your body, soul, and mind.
  - Don't fail to get inoculations. Preventive medicine will save you from sick time.
  - Don't overindulge in bad diets. Healthy eating keeps you healthy and time-efficient.
  - Don't search for love in the wrong places. Time is wasted on wrong endeavors.
- Practice good personal habits:
  - Eat well.
  - Love well. This is the tonic for body and mind.
  - Visit your doctor regularly. This helps to keep you well and time-efficient.
- Have a plan and execute your plan.
- Socialize without going overboard.

Tips for Student Application of the 8-by-3 Model:

- Sleep well; it reinvigorates the brain so that it requires less time to learn.
- Pay attention in class the first time; there will not be enough time to do it later.
- Manage your time upfront; time is irrecoverable once it is lost.

- Don't go to class late; it will cost you more time to catch up with class later on.
- Don't text, talk, or doodle in class; what you miss in class will cost more time to learn.
- Don't turn in homework late; it costs less time to do it on time and forget it.
- Study incrementally rather than in overextended blocks of time. Smaller chunks of knowledge stick better and longer.
- Allocate a bounded and limited time for friends; they can occupy your time needlessly.
- Avoid frivolous pursuits; they divert your time from meaningful activities.
- Develop and maintain good work ethics; keeping to tasks costs less time.
- Demonstrate good personal ethics; doing the right time costs less time.
- Avoid instant gratification; it comes back to bite your time later on.
- Develop a sustainable schedule for studying; a consistent study pattern requires less time.
- Recognize that education is power; invest your time in getting it at the earliest opportunity.
- Commit the quote below to your heart:

> "Education is the most powerful weapon which you
> can use to change the world." – Nelson Mandela

Get actively involved in learning opportunities. Direct involvement seals the deal of learning. Adopt the philosophy below:

> "Tell me and I forget;
> Show me and I remember;
> Involve me and I understand."
> - Confucius, Chinese Philosopher

As with any new approach, acceptance and embrace are keys to the success of the approach. The 8-by-3 paradigm is new and different from conventional approaches to managing time. A fair assessment of the strengths and weaknesses of any approach can help users make a better decision on how to embrace and utilize the new approach. The table below presents the pros and cons of the 8-by-3 model. An implementation of the new paradigm may at first appear to be difficult and overly structured. Indeed, it can be hard to be structured in these days of a rushed society and crowded lifestyles. But, as Author Thomas Carlyle reminds us, "Every noble work is at first impossible." So, give it a try and you'll be amazed how well this new paradigm can aid your time management.

Using DEJI Systems Model

Using a systems-thinking approach can help in saving time. The goal is to discover potential areas of impacting consistency in our actions. Systems engineering is a good and proven tool for ensuring operational efficiency, effectiveness, and consistency. There are many models of systems engineering used in business and industry. These models are predicated on the following definition of a system.

A system is a collection of interrelated elements, whose collective output (impact) together is higher than the mere sum of the individual outputs of the elements.

In order to save time, activities are best performed in a systematic way, such that a sustainable process is achieved. The DEJI (Design, Evaluation, Justification, Integration) Systems Model is designed to ensure that a structured and systematic pathway to the end goal is maintained. The effort begins with job design and the structured process goes through the following stages:

- **Design** of action
  Design, in this case, could be a plan, a purpose, a scheme, a strategy, an intension, and so on.
- **Evaluation** of the design
- **Justification** of the design
- **Integration** of the design
  Integration, in this case, is the alignment of the design into normal operation This is the best way to sustain the intended accomplishment.

We cannot change humans. So, we must design our actions around human attributes. In order words, we must integrate desired actions and outputs with the typical human attributes and capabilities. If this can be done, time can be saved at every stage of the process. The DEJI systems model is unique among process improvement tools and techniques because it explicitly calls for a justification of the product within the process improvement cycle. This is important for the purpose of determining when a program should be terminated even after going into production. If the program is justified, it must then be integrated and "accepted" within the ongoing business of the enterprise. The DEJI model facilitates such a recursive design-evaluate-justify-integrate process for enterprise feedback looping. The biggest challenge for any project management endeavor is coordinating and integrating the multiple facets that affect the final outputs of a project, where a specific output may be a physical product, a service, or a desired result. Addressing the challenges of project execution from a systems perspective increases the likelihood of success. The DEJI model can facilitate project success through structural implementation. Although originally developed for product development projects, the model is generally applicable to all types of time-affecting endeavors as illustrated in the figure below. The model can be applied across the spectrum of the following elements of any organization:

- People
- Process
- Technology

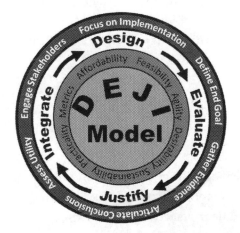

Design Stage of DEJI

Product or process design should be structured to follow point-to-point transformation. A good technique to accomplish this is the use of state-space transformation, with which we can track the evolution of a project from concept stage to final product stage. For the purpose of project management, we adopt the general definitions and characteristics of state-space modeling. A state is a set of conditions that describe a process at a specified point in time.

A project *state-space* is the set of all possible states of the project lifecycle. State-space representation can solve project design problems by moving from an initial state to another state, and eventually to a goal state. The movement from state to state is achieved by means of actions. A goal is a description of an intended state that has not yet been achieved. The process of solving a project problem involves finding a sequence of actions that represents a solution path from the initial state to the goal state. A state-space model consists of state variables that describe the prevailing condition of the project. The state variables are related to inputs by mathematical relationships. Examples of potential project state variables include schedule, output quality, cost, due date, resource, manpower utilization, and productivity level.

Evaluation Stage of DEJI

A project can be evaluated on the basis of cost, quality, and performance. Several quantitative techniques are available for the evaluation stage. Examples include learning curve analysis, cost-benefit analysis, earned-value analysis, and rate-of-return analysis.

Justification Stage of DEJI

We need to justify actions on the basis of quantitative-value assessment. The systems value model is a good quantitative technique that can be used for action justification on the basis of value. The model provides a heuristic decision aid for comparing action alternatives.

Integration Stage of DEJI

Without being integrated, a system will be in isolation and it may be worthless. We must integrate all the elements of a system on the basis of alignment of functional goals. The overlap of systems for integration purposes can conceptually be viewed as projection integrals by considering areas bounded by the common elements of the sub-systems. In the final analysis, creating the virtual twenty-fifth hour in the day implies saving time in executing every action at the various steps in the pursuit of our daily goals. The premise of this book is to provide tips and guidance for getting more done each day through a more effective use of time. Time saved is akin to time gained. Thus, the concept of creating a virtual twenty-fifth hour in the day presents the essence of using every minute more effectively. Managing time requires dedication and commitment. Occasional drifting away from time-management goals is okay, but a wholesale abandonment of the lessons learned in this book will be a disservice to self and mission.

My recommendation to readers is to develop the habit of constantly exploring opportunities for time-management improvement. There is always room for improvement. As such, good things can be made to be even better. Preemption of time robbers is one essential approach to executing the creation of the virtual twenty-fifth hour. One common flaw in human operations is the focus on the regrets of time that we have already lost. The recommended approach of this book is to focus more on the time that we don't yet have. By doing so, we can identify (in advance) and mitigate potential time distractions. With all these, we can remind ourselves that haste makes waste. Upfront care preempts the need for haste.

The concept of lean operations is effective for managing current and future activities. Lean means the identification and elimination of sources of waste in operations. We recall that Six Sigma involves the identification and elimination of source of defects. A defect, in this context, requires a repair, a re-work, or a re-do, which consumes more time unnecessarily. When Lean and Six Sigma are coupled, an organization can derive the double benefit of reducing waste and defects in operations, which leads to what is known as Lean-Six-Sigma. Consequently, we can achieve higher output, better performance, better satisfaction of requirements, and more effective utilization of limited resources, particularly time. The basic principle of "lean" is to take a close look at the elemental compositions of a process so that non-value-adding elements can be located and eliminated. That is the underlying principles of saving time to create the virtual twenty-fifth hour in the day.

I wish readers well in adopting, adapting, and complying with the guidance and tips provided in this book. Happy time execution!

CHAPTER 12

CONCLUSION: CLOSING THOUGHTS

Time is of the essence in everything we do. He or she, who manages time well will have more discretionary time to get more done each day. This is how I have managed my personal time for many years. The successes that I have enjoyed in my own time management strategies provide the impetus for me to share the tips and techniques presented in this book with others. Hence, the readers of this book have seen, first-hand, how time management has helped me and they can emulate the guidance to do likewise.

Time management is the major component of project management. The other components of cost and quality can only be achieved if time is available. Thus, time, as a factor of project performance, is of utmost importance. All the tools and techniques presented in this book come together to form the basis for a better project management. A successful project management is manifested through the project schedule, which is the commitment of resources against time.

Consider the centuries-old quote below:

"We trained hard, but it seemed that every time we were beginning to form into teams, we would be reorganized.

I was to learn later in life that we tend to meet any new situations by reorganizing; and what a wonderful method it can be for creating the illusion of progress while producing confusion, inefficiency, and demoralization." – Petronius Arbiter, 210 BC

Lesson learned from the quote is that if you want results, you must use project management. Every organization wants more results in less time with fewer resources. It is through the structured approach of project management that an organization can overcome confusion, inefficiency, and demoralization. Every organization needs project management! Everyone needs project management! The application of project management is vital in business, industry, government, and personal activities. Everyone needs project management because projects offer an avenue for the accomplishment of human effort. The core competence that employers require of new hires most often include leadership, team skills, and project management.

So often is project management required in an organization that most now use Management-By-Projects (MBP) as a primary business strategy. Contemporary economy is built on service enterprises, such as IT services, product design services, and supply chain. Many of such services are conducted on a project basis. The formal definition below explains the importance of MBP in organizations. Management-By-Projects (MBP) facilitates an application of the multi-dimensionality of factors that influence the accomplishment of organizational goals. MBP has several benefits. It helps the process of learning leadership practices, team building, employee relations, interpersonal skills, and communication skills. Most projects have the same things in common:

- People Issues
- Resource Shortage
- Time Crunch

Project principles, similarities, and practices are transferable across industries, across cultures, and across geographical boundaries. This makes MBP very versatile and generally applicable to different organization sizes, shapes, and locations. The vision and mission of a project will dictate the process of applying project management concepts, tools, and techniques in pursuit of organizational goals. The samples that follow are indicative of the need to create an operational platform for each project. In achieving the objectives of MBP, an organization must have a succinct vision for the project of interest and a clear mission statement to accomplish the project goals. A vision statement says how things ought to be for the future while a mission statement indicates how things are currently.

In project management, people issues are fuzzy, ambiguous, and subject to emotional nuances and sentimental knee-jerk reactions. Consequently, the people side of project management requires more managerial care because no mathematical prescriptions are available to manage people.

The primary implementations of project management center around qualitative, quantitative, and computer techniques. Each of these has been extensively addressed independently and collectively in many publications. A common mistake is to quickly jump to computer implementation because computer tools for project management have become very accessible in recent years. The fact is that computer implementations cannot succeed without appropriate qualitative analysis and quantitative modeling. Project success rests on the "shoulders" of people. That is, people as project team members; people as project owners; or people as project customers. Qualitative analysis must precede quantitative analysis, before computer analysis can succeed.

The techniques of project management have become major tools used to accomplish goals and objectives. Project management, as a body of knowledge, is reshaping business processes. A strategic plan cannot be realized until the process of project management is applied to implement the tactical objectives of the plan. The term "project management" generally implies the broad conceptual approached used to manage projects within the constraints of time, cost, and performance expectations. Project management has proven very useful in different types of endeavors. Diverse areas such as engineering, construction, social work, health services, research, business, marketing, and education have benefited from the application of project management techniques. Management-by-projects offers a huge competitive advantage for companies and a personal benefit for individuals.

The practice of project management continues to grow at an astronomical pace. This growth is evidenced by the present membership size of the Project Management Institute (PMI), the international professional organization for project management. The global appeal and relevance of project management has created many professional opportunities for practitioners, consultants, and researchers. This leads to the need for simple and practical guide books. This book focuses on time management as the basis for project management. Modern projects encompass a lot more than activity management. This author expanded the conventional view of a project by offering an alternate definition of project management, which says:

> "Project management is the process of managing, allocating, and timing resources to achieve a given goal in an efficient and expeditious manner."

This expanded definition permits the incorporation of swiftness and expediency to the conventional perception of project management. Project goals are achieved through an integrative synergy between people, tools, and process. As the integral component of project efforts, human resources should enjoy a high priority in an organization's strategic plans. If an organization treats its workforce with dignity, it will bring out the best in the workers, both individually and as a group. Project life cycle revolves around several factors that define the overall utility of the project. My concluding thought for this book is that if you have good time management, you will have good project management. This book is designed to help you in that respect. Happy reading and reviewing.

Chapter 12 References

1. Badiru, A. B. (2008), **Triple C Model of Project Management: Communication, Cooperation, and Coordination**, Taylor & Francis CRC Press, Boca Raton, FL, 2008.
2. Badiru, A. B. (2019), **Project Management: Systems, Principles, and Applications**, Second Edition, Taylor & Francis CRC Press, Boca Raton, FL, 2019.

APPENDIX A

DEJI BADIRU'S QUIPS AND QUOTES

"Life is to be lived with new challenges." - Adedeji Badiru

"Life is lived and sustained through new challenges." – Adedeji Badiru

"Scholarship does not make leadership." – Adedeji Badiru

"What you have the right to do is not always the right thing to do." – Adedeji Badiru

"Management should not always do what management has the right to do." – Deji Badiru

"Duty is a responsibility, employment is a necessity." – Adedeji Badiru

"Every failure represents an acquisition of experience to get us ready for the next success." – Adedeji Badiru

"The only way to learn a permanent lesson is to confront and correct errors." – Adedeji Badiru

"When curiosity is established, the urge to learn develops." - Adedeji Badiru

"Education misapplied is education missed." – Adedeji Badiru

"If the snail is moving, at least we know it is moving." – Adedeji Badiru

"If you wait long enough, you won't have to buy new technology." - Adedeji Badiru

"While we are bickering on little things, bigger things are eating our lunch." –Adedeji Badiru

"The door of opportunity that is half open needs a push or pull from the other side." – Adedeji Badiru

"He who is married to the numbers cannot appreciate the beauty of what generated the numbers." – Adedeji Badiru

Motto: "Family first, job always" – Adedeji Badiru

"Friendship does not discriminate." – Adedeji Badiru

"Sharp as shadow's edge." - Adedeji Badiru

"Harm can come from the harmless." – Adedeji Badiru

"For better, together; for worse, divided." – Adedeji Badiru

"It is more difficult to sustain an improvement change than it is to initiate it." Adedeji Badiru

"Spring has sprung and summer is yet to come." – Adedeji Badiru

"Problems cannot be wished away. Like weeds, if not controlled, they grow uncontrollably." – Adedeji Badiru

"I'd be more of a handicap than a handy-man in an unfamiliar game." – Adedeji Badiru

"You can get out and be somebody or stay in and be homebody." – Adedeji Badiru

"The joy of traveling is coming back home." - Adedeji Badiru

"Speed reading is the flip side of speed writing." – Adedeji Badiru

"New love is like new alcohol; it makes you lose your senses." – Adedeji Badiru

"Fiction is the outcome of a writer's warped mind." – Adedeji Badiru

"Tradition is a strand of culture." – Adedeji Badiru

"Beware of the clash of gastronomic aroma at the buffet table." – Adedeji Badiru

"The flame of desire has seared his deepest veins." – Adedeji Badiru

"The recipes that become extinct are those that have not learned to adapt to human palate." – Adedeji Badiru

"Sweeten two pots with only one drop of honey." – Adedeji Badiru

"It is funny how the mind of a writer works; contoured and tortured with expressive words." – Adedeji Badiru

"Food is essential for a good life, but too much of a good life is a death sentence." – Adedeji Badiru

"The host country is the labor of existence while the fun in the home country is the fruit of labor." – Adedeji Badiru

"Sustainability requires communication, cooperation, and coordination on a bedrock of commitment and discipline." – Adedeji Badiru

"If this event piques your interest, then pick a time to take a peek at the peck on the peak of his beak." – Adedeji Badiru

"You are, indeed, the candle that lights the way of angels" – Adedeji original

"Only bad decisions make good stories" – Adedeji Badiru

"Each day is a better day because it adds to the overall longevity." – Adedeji Badiru

"A systems view of the world is what is required to keep industry well oiled." – Adedeji Badiru

"On the critical path, the shortest distance between two poor points is a curve." – Adedeji Badiru

"It is your job to do your job. It is my job to promote your job." – Adedeji Badiru

"I am an engineer; I figure things out." – Adedeji Badiru

"Please don't congra-too-late me; it is too late." – Adedeji Badiru

"Talk expands to fill the available time." – Adedeji Badiru

"My creaky knees are reminding me of how many miles they've logged over the past decades."

"Win or lose, we are winners because we survive."

"When a wife says to her husband, 'will kill you', don't believe a word of it." – Adedeji Badiru

"When a husband says to his wife, 'I will kill you', you'd better watch out." – Adedeji Badiru

Another Chicken Joke
Q: "Who is notified when a fellow dies in the coop?"
A: "Next of Chicken"

"If all the leaders of the world were women, they would spend more time talking and less time fighting." – Adedeji Badiru

Wonderment Quips
"Politics without potential puzzles me."
"Passion without protection perplexes me."
"Rhetoric without result repulses me."
"Confrontation without conscience confuses me."
"Bragging without basis baffles me."
"Accolades without impact amazes me."
"Involvement without influence infuriates me."

"The better a person you are, the poorer a pauper you will be." – Adedeji Badiru

"The kinder a person you are, the poorer you will b." – Adedeji Badiru

"A dead person doesn't miss what he is missing." – Adedeji Badiru

"Whoever is dead doesn't miss whatever he is missing." – Adedeji Badiru

"Some dictators move people from oppression to suppression." – Adedeji Badiru

"Don't kill yourself before death arrives at your doorstep." – Adedeji Badiru

"I can control only what is within my control." – Adedeji Badiru

"Don't get frustrated, get inspired." – Adedeji Badiru

"I don't give excuses and I don't give up." – Adedeji Badiru

"What I saw, I saw, with my saw in hand." – Adedeji Badiru

"Don't shy away from challenges; nothing develops a person better than adversity." – Adedeji Badiru

"I don't criticize, I critique." – Adedeji Badiru

Stories come with age.

"I have nothing against rich people, if they would just leave me alone and stop asking me for more money" – Adedeji Badiru

"Every new challenge is a learning opportunity." – Adedeji Badiru

"You are as old as the mirror tells you you are." – Adedeji Badiru

"Even after death, life continues and bills continue." – Adedeji Badiru

"My philosophy is that what is worth doing is worth doing well and worth doing promptly." – Adedeji Badiru

"What matters more is what we do with our scholarship rather than what our scholarship is." – Adedeji Badiru

"I put honey on the brownie and I got brawny and brainy." – Adedeji Badiru

"The most sustainable wealth is the wealth that is accumulated over the long haul." – Adedeji Badiru

"Nature has a twisted sense of humor. Whatever is good for our taste buds is never good for our body." - Adedeji Badiru

"If there is a reason for everything, everything will have a reason for every season, which is clearly not the case." – Adedeji Badiru

"Enjoy the present, but exercise caution. Look outward to the future, but respect the past. Look hopefully to the future and honor the past. Look longingly to the future, but learn respectfully from the past." – Adedeji Badiru

He snatched him from the jaw of poverty.

Education is what is needed to rescue us from the jaws of poverty.

"A distended stomach that is pumped full of rice needs some ice to temper it." – Adedeji Badiru

"You don't really understand anything until you have looked at everything from many different perspectives." – Adedeji Badiru

"If you want something done prompt and proper, you have to process it yourself." – Adedeji Badiru

"Patchwork never works." – Adedeji Badiru

"Every little help helps every time." – Adedeji Badiru

"Never give bad a chance, or it will overshadow good." – Adedeji Badiru

"If it is your work, proclaim it, protect it, project it, promote it. – Adedeji Badiru

"I don't like hanging around work. I prefer getting rid of it as soon as it shows up in my presence." – Adedeji Badiru

"I hate lingering work. I get rid of work as soon as it comes my way." – Adedeji Badiru

"Sustainable success lies in what we do rather than what we say." – Adedeji Badiru

"The loudest first cricket gets the first attention." – Adedeji Badiru

"A mountain by any other name does not diminish its peak." – Adedeji Badiru

"The prestige of a University is measured by the accomplishments of the faculty." – Adedeji Badiru

"Take care of your faculty and staff so that they will take care of the students!" – Adedeji Badiru

Family Legacy: "What to leave for your children is a legacy of integrity, dignity, respect, discipline, and honest rather than a litany of worldly materials." – Adedeji Badiru

"Please put Principles above personality and process above product. We need to value the process above the product of the process. Products will change; they will come and go; but the integrity and value of the process must be sustained." – Adedeji Badiru

"I get done what needs to be done." – Adedeji Badiru

"Organizational bureaucracy can impede intellectual agility." – Adedeji Badiru

"Apple Pickers Picket at the Pickle Park." – Adedeji Badiru

"Things sweet to plan can prove in execution to be a dud of a flop." 27 August 2016

"Q: Why are movers' schedules undependable? A: They are always on the move." – Adedeji Badiru

"He creates the fire that he shouts to fight" – Adedeji Badiru

"We must temper idealism with reality." – Adedeji Badiru

"Happy-Go-Working People; They work better when they are happy." – Adedeji Badiru

"We thrive together when we tie our work together." – Adedeji Badiru

"Working together productively requires that the work be designed to permit teamwork." – Adedeji Badiru

"In teamwork, we work and thrive so that our work works well for us and others." – Adedeji Badiru

"The alternative to happiness is not pleasant." – Adedeji Badiru

"Do what you enjoy doing as an avocation that makes you happy. It lengthens the richness of your life. Of what use is a life of worldly riches devoid of richness of life?" – Adedeji Badiru

"The reality of life is death; "The reality of death is just a stone throw away." – Adedeji Badiru

"Avoid hurried worries in harried times." – Adedeji Badiru

"A sitting duck is plum for the plucking." – Adedeji Badiru

"Lesson learned should be lesson practiced." – Adedeji Badiru

"Don't use people as rungs for your ladder of ego." – Adedeji Badiru

"If you want to get there faster, you should start earlier." – Adedeji Badiru

"If we wait until everything is well aligned before we do something, we will never do anything." – Adedeji Badiru

"Nothing is perfect, no one is perfect. We should continue to tweak a process toward continuous improvement." – Adedeji Badiru

"A man becomes well-known for his wise words and sage sayings rather than his ego." – Adedeji Badiru

"If it weren't for people, the work environment would be a great place to work." – Adedeji Badiru

"Whenever opportunity knocks, we must venture out to grab it." – Adedeji Badiru

"Success in life should be gaged by the success of those you help to succeed, and not by your own success of assets." – Adedeji Badiru

"If you are starving, every bite of any food is mouth-watering." – Adedeji Badiru

"Invest ten minutes of proper planning to get one hour of time savings." – Adedeji Badiru

"Penny in, pound out is the way to grow a sustainable wealth." – Adedeji Badiru

"Don't scurry into a hole or scamper off stage just because things are difficult. It is in difficulty that success is forged." – Adedeji Badiru

"Not everything that is feasible is practical and desirable." – Adedeji Badiru

"Where there is no measurement, there can be no standard." – Adedeji Badiru

"Measurement mitigates mess-ups." – Adedeji Badiru

"Pandemonic is what happens when a demon causes a pandemonium with a pandemic." – Adedeji Badiru

"Data viewed is data appreciated." – Adedeji Badiru

"Believe me or not, the data tells you the facts." – Adedeji Badiru

"Where there is no calculation, there is no compliance." – Adedeji Badiru

"Statistics is the language of data." – Adedeji Badiru

"What you see is what the data says." – Adedeji Badiru

"A model is worth a thousand narratives." – Adedeji Badiru

"If there is no integration, there is no implementation." Adedeji Badiru

"When the population overwhelms the infrastructure, what results is chaos." – Adedeji Badiru

"To be prepared is to be confident." – Adedeji Badiru

"If you think you are strong, use the strength to lift someone up rather than using it to knock people down." - Adedeji Badiru

"Home is where the heart is; Wife is what makes the home." – Adedeji Badiru

"If it is a hard nut to crack, please, by all means, use a sledge hammer." – Adedeji Badiru

"If you do good, show others how it is done so that your legacy can be perpetuated." – Adedeji Badiru

"The claw of that clause is to scratch the surface of the facts." – Adedeji Badiru

"Just because shit came from you doesn't mean you should take it back in." – Adedeji Badiru

"Sustainable success lies in what we do rather than what we say." – Adedeji Badiru

"The loudest cricket gets the first attention." – Adedeji Badiru

"Haste makes waste, just as rush makes ruin." – Adedeji Badiru

"A safe time is the best time." – Adedeji Badiru

"With togetherness, we progress together." – Adedeji Badiru

"Dreams of impossibility can become possible with positivity." – Adedeji Badiru

"For operational excellence, I prefer problem preemption over problem correction." – Adedeji Badiru

Quip: "Planetary physics is about a white mass in a black hole." – Adedeji Badiru

"Those who love to cook must stir the pot periodically." – Adedeji Badiru

"You cannot be so good that no one else is as good." – Adedeji Badiru

"You know you are on a path to greatness if you discover changeable deficiencies in your approach without anyone prompting you." – Adedeji Badiru

"We should not be doing more work all the time. Rather, we should be doing more things smartly all the time." – Adedeji Badiru

"If health is wealth, how much capital investment and reinvestment have you committed to your health?" – Adedeji Badiru

"No health, no work. No work, no wealth." – Adedeji Badiru

"Where time goes, cost follows." – Adedeji Badiru

"You must know where your long-gone cost is buried." Adedeji Badiru

"Preemption of time robbers is better than correction of time robbers." Adedeji Badiru, 2020

"The nucleus of a task is in splitting it in two." – Adedeji Badiru

"No wisdom is lost from removing wisdom teeth." – Adedeji Badiru

"Success is a function of intelligence, common sense, and self-discipline." – Adedeji Badiru

"The grass is always greener where you most need it to be dead." – Adedeji Badiru

"Invest today in what will benefit you tomorrow." – Adedeji Badiru

"Success comes from self-discipline." – Adedeji Badiru

"To get more done, try and do less." – Adedeji Badiru

"Get it done and put it behind you." – Adedeji Badiru

"Divide and conquer works for getting things done." – Adedeji Badiru

"Communication is the root of everything else." – Adedeji Badiru

"A map is the plan of the wise." – Adedeji Badiru

"Resource is the engine of performance." – Adedeji Badiru

"Let common sense be the guiding light for getting things done." – Adedeji Badiru

"Do not do in the dark what is best done in daylight hours." – Adedeji Badiru

"Do not waste daylight hours doing things that are best done after sunset." – Adedeji Badiru

"Time is the controller of everything." – Adedeji Badiru

"To get things done promptly, organize, organize, and organize again." – Adedeji Badiru

"A systems view of the world is what keeps the wheel of performance well oiled." – Adedeji Badiru

"Early to bed, early to rise is the secret of time management to get more done each day." – Adedeji Badiru

APPENDIX B

TIME-RELEVANT CONVERSION FACTORS

"Time is the controller of every conversion."
– Adedeji Badiru

A. Temperature conversion factors

Conversion formulas

Celsius to Kelvin $K = C + 273.15$

Celsius to Fahrenheit $F = (9/5)C + 32$

Fahrenheit to Celsius $C = (5/9)(F - 32)$

Fahrenheit to Kelvin $K = (5/9)(F + 459.67)$

Fahrenheit to Rankin $R = F + 459.67$

Rankin to Kelvin $K = (5/9)R$

The time of day affects the expected temperature.

B. Kitchen Measurement Conversion Factors

1 pinch	= 1/8 tea spoon or less
3 tea spoons	= 1 table spoon
2 table spoons	= 1/8 cup
4 table spoons	= 1/4 cup
8 table spoons	= 1/2 cup
12 table spoons	= 3/4 cup
16 table spoons	= 1 cup
5 table spoons + 1 tea spoon	= 1/3 cup
4oz	= 1/2 cup
8oz	= 1 cup
16 oz	= 1lb
1 oz	= 2 table spoons of fat or liquid
1 cup of liquid	= 1/2 pint
2 cups	= 1 pint
2 pints	= 1 quart
4 cup of liquid	= 1 quart
4 quarts	= 1 gallon
8 quarts	= 1 peck (apples, pears, etc.)
1 jigger	= 1½ fluid oz
1 jigger	= 3 table spoons

Time spent in the kitchen is affected by measurement translations.

C. Micro and Macro Number Notations

Notations and Expansions

yotta (10^{24}):   1, 000, 000, 000, 000, 000, 000, 000, 000

zetta (10^{21}):   1, 000, 000, 000, 00,0 000, 000, 000

exa (10^{18}):   1, 000, 000, 000, 000, 000, 000

peta (10^{15}):   1, 000, 000, 000, 000, 000

tera (10^{12}):   1, 000, 000, 000, 000

giga (10^{9}):   1, 000, 000, 000

mega (10^{6}):   1, 000, 000

kilo (10^3): 1, 000
hecto (10^2): 100
deca (10^1): 10
deci (10^{1}): 0.1
centi (10^{-2}): 0.01
milli (10^{-3}): 0.001
micro (10^{-6}): 0.000 001
nano (10^{-9}): 0.000 000 001
pico (10^{-12}): 0.000 000 000 001
femto (10^{-15}): 0.000 000 000 000 001
atto (10^{-18}): 0.000 000 000 000 000 001
zepto (10^{-21}): 0.000 000 000 000 000 000 001
yocto (10^{-24}): 0.000 000 000 000 000 000 000 001
stringo (10^{-35}): 0.000 000 000 000 000 000 000 000 000 000 000 01

Measurement of time requirement may range from tiny to huge, as in nanosecond and light-year time scales.

D. Decimal Conversion

1/16 = 0.0625
1/8 = .125
3/16 = .1875
1/4 = .25
5/16 = .3125
3/8 = .375
7/16 = .4375
½ = .5
9/16 = .5625
5/8 = .625
11/16 = .6875
3/4 = .75
13/16 =.8125
7/8 = .875
15/16 = .9375
1 = 1.0

Fraction of time implies time sensitivity, as in split-second.

E. Distance Measurement

English system
1 foot (ft) = 12 inches (in)
1 yard (yd) = 3 feet
1 mile (mi) = 1,760 yards
1 sq. foot = 144 sq. inches
1 sq. yard = 9 sq. feet
1 acre = 4,840 sq. yards = 43,560 sq. feet
1 sq. mile = 640 acres

Metric system
mm = Millimeter (.001m)
cm = Centimeter (.01m)
dm = Decimeter (.1m)
m = Meter (1m)
dam = Decameter (10m)
hm = Hectometer (100m)
km = Kilometer (1,000m)
Coverage of distance takes time, as in miles per hour.

F. Distance Conversion

feet = 0.30480 meters = 12 inches
inches = 25.40 millimeters = 0.02540 meters = 0.08333 feet
kilometers = 3,280.8 feet = 0.6214 miles = 1,094 yards
meters = 39.370 inches = 3.2808 feet = 1.094 yards
miles = 5,280 feet = 1.6093 kilometers = 0.8694 nautical miles
millimeters = 0.03937 inches
nautical miles = 6,076 feet = 1.852 kilometers
yards = 0.9144 meters = 3 feet = 36 inches
The passage of time assures the coverage of distance.

G. Velocity conversion factors

feet/minute = 5.080 mm/second
feet/second = 0.3048 meters/second

inches/second = 0.0254 meters/second
km/hour = 0.6214 miles/hour
meters/second = 3.2808 feet/second = 2.237 miles/hour
miles/hour = 88.0 feet/minute = 0.44704 meters/second = 1.6093 km/
hour = 0.8684 knots
knot = 1.151 miles/hour
Velocity is Distance over Time.

H. Volume conversion factors

acre-foot = 1,233.5 cubic meters
cubic cm = 0.06102 cubic inches
cubic feet = 1,728 cu. inches = 7.480 gallons (US) = 0.02832 cu. meters =
0.03704 cu. Yards
liter = 1.057 = liquid quarts = 0.908 dry quarts = 61.024 cubic inches
gallons (US) = 231 cu. in = 3.7854 liters = 4 quarts = 0.833 British gallons
= 128 US fluid oz.
quarts(US) = 0.9463 liters
Flow rate per unit time is related to volume, as in flood rate.

I. Time-related Energy Conversion

BTU = 1,055.9 joules = 0.2520 kg-calories
Watt-hour = 3,600 joules = 3.409 BTU
HP (electric) = 746 watts
BTU/second = 1,055.9 watts
Watt-second = 1 joule
Energy consumption is a function of time, as in watts per second.

J. Time-based constants

Speed of light = $2.997,925 \times 10^{10}$ cm/sec = 983.6×10^6 ft/sec = 186,284 miles/sec
Velocity of sound = 340.3 meters/sec = 1116 ft/sec
Gravity (acceleration) = 9.80665 m/sec square = 32.174 ft/sec square
386.089 inches/sec square
The passage of time is constant.

Printed in the United States
by Baker & Taylor Publisher Services